BLACKWOOD ON SLAMS

BLACKWOOD ON SLAMS

Easley Blackwood

♠ ♡ ◇ ♣

PRENTICE-HALL, INC., Englewood Cliffs, N.J.

Prentice-Hall International, Inc., *London*
Prentice-Hall of Australia, Pty. Ltd., *Sydney*
Prentice-Hall of Canada, Ltd., *Toronto*
Prentice-Hall of India Private Ltd., *New Delhi*
Prentice-Hall of Japan, Inc., *Tokyo*

Introduction

The name "Blackwood" is more often used than any other in the game of contract bridge—and the slam bidding convention he invented is more often invoked in vain. Many players seem to feel that there is something sinful in getting to a slam without using Easley Blackwood's 4-5 Notrump Convention on the way; the fact is that he introduced it in order to help players avoid bidding slams that wouldn't make.

Of course, there is no such thing as patenting a bid and collecting a royalty on it, but if Blackwood had a nickel for every time his bid was properly used he'd be a rich man indeed; if he had a nickel for every time it was misused, he'd be a multi-millionaire. Not that anyone need be concerned about the financial status of the highly successful insurance executive who retired early in order to travel, only to be hauled back into action as Executive Secretary and General Manager of the American Contract Bridge League, to resolve the major problems that faced the world's largest and most influential bridge organization.

Like all successful executives, Blackwood can always find time to do an essential job, which is why he has produced this book to help resolve the major problems that face the world's bridge players—how to enjoy and profit from the most exciting bids in bridge . . . SLAMS.

RICHARD L. FREY

Contents

1. Introduction to Slam-Bidding and Play 1
2. The Blackwood Convention 3
   Asking for Aces 5
   Asking for Kings 6
   The Rule of One and Two 7
   Second- and Third-Round Controls 8
   Playing at 5 NT 9
   Showing Voids 10
   When Opponents Interfere 14
   Importance of the Queen of Trumps 15
3. The Gerber 4 ♣ Convention 19
   Regular Use of Gerber 19
   Gerber in Unusual Situations 24
4. Cue-Bidding for Slams 27
   Sequence of Cue-Bids 28
   Cue-Bidding to Show Second-Round Control 29
   Cue-Bidding to Reach 3 NT 35
   Five-Level Asking Bids 37
   Blackwood After Cue-Bidding 38
5. When Is Blackwood Blackwood? 41
   4 NT as a Notrump Raise 42
   4 NT as the Unusual Notrump 43
   Effect of Opponent's Preempt 48
   More Examples of 4 NT Bids 49
   Summing Up the Problem 51
6. Point Count vs. Playing Tricks 53
   Need to Determine Playing Tricks 53
   An Example of Drastic Revaluation 55
   Taking Maximum Action 60
   Counting Controls 61
   Secondary Advantage of High Cards 63

7. Bidding to Slam   65
    The Direct Method of Slam-Bidding   65
    Practicing Economy in the Bidding   68
    Watch Out for Misfits   71
    Unscientific Slam-Bidding   73
    Unusual Slam Tries   75

8. Slam-Bidding After Opening 1 NT   79
    History of the Notrump Bid   79
    The Fifteen to Seventeen Point Notrump   80

9. Notrump Slams   85
    Point Count and Notrump Slams   87
    Considerations Other than Aces and Kings   88

10. The In-Between Hand   93

11. Action After a Game-Level Jump Response   97

12. Grand Slams   103
    Grand-Slam Force   105
    Variations of the Grand-Slam Force   108

13. Arithmetic of a Slam   111
    Grand-Slam Arithmetic   111
    Small-Slam Arithmetic   112

14. Defending Against Slams   113
    When *Not* to Double   114
    The Lightner Slam Double   116
    Variation of the Lightner Slam Double   120
    Doubling a Blackwood Response   121
    Doubling "on General Principles"   125
    Opening Leads Against Slams   128
    Leading an Ace Against Slams   133
    Leading Against a Grand Slam   135

15. Slam Play   139
    Losing a Trick to Set Up a Squeeze   139
    Losing a Trick to Entice a Favorable Lead   142
    Losing a Trick to Ensure the Contract   145
    Losing a Trick as a Safety Measure   146

16. The Humanics of Slam-Bidding   151

BLACKWOOD ON SLAMS

1

Introduction to Slam-Bidding and Play

♠ ♡ ◇ ♣

Bidding and making a slam can be the biggest thrill in the game of bridge. For the dedicated tournament player there is the deep personal satisfaction of bringing the contract home after being on thin ice all the way, the plaudits of partner and even, on rare occasions, the grudging approval of the opponents. For the more sporting type of player who indulges in bridge for something more than the mere love of it, there is the substantial monetary reward.

This book is designed to show you three things: How to reach slams that can be made or, at worst, have an odds-on chance; how to stay out of slams that cannot be made; and how to defend in those sour situations when your opponents bid slams.

One extremely important word should be mentioned at the start, and you will find it again and again throughout the book. The word is *controls*. This simply means the ability to win the first or second round of any suit the defenders choose to lead.

For example, consider these partnership hands:

WEST	EAST
♠ 5 4	♠ 9 7
♡ A K Q 9 7 6	♡ J 10
◇ J 10 9	◇ A K Q 8 7 6
♣ A 2	♣ K Q 9

Let us say that West is playing a contract of 7 ♡. If he had the choice of the opening lead he could make a grand slam. But apparently this partnership overlooked the somewhat irritating section of the rules that say the opening lead belongs to the defending side. The defenders, of course, promptly cashed two spade tricks. The East-West combination lacked the necessary controls for even a small slam.

Controls give you time to work out the hand in your favor, and the element of *time* increases tremendously in importance as the bidding proceeds to the higher levels. Say you are in a contract of 3 NT, and by perfect play you could make four-odd. But actually you are a little careless and make only three. Well, except in a duplicate game, this will not be a disaster—you have lost only a paltry thirty points. However, in a small-slam contract there is no place for this devil-may-care attitude. You have very little time to be careless. And of course, in a grand slam you have no time at all.

Three main types of slam-bidding will be presented in the following pages. They are:

The Blackwood Convention
The Gerber Convention
Cue-bids

You need to know how to use all three, because each applies to certain types of hands and is a losing proposition with other types.

One other thought: Do not be a slave to *any* convention. Leave a little common sense and good judgment in the game. You will feel freer, and you will probably win more.

2

The Blackwood Convention

♠ ♡ ◇ ♣

If asked to name the single most important element of usefulness of the Blackwood Slam Convention, my answer would be: It keeps you out of unmakeable slams. Helping to reach slams that *are* makable would be only secondary.

That nebulous character commonly known as "the average player" feels called upon to bound into 4 NT at the very first scent of a slam. Usually he will have a good hand and his partner will have shown strength. But this is not enough.

Let us say that a partnership has 33 high-card points. Very good. Since there are only 40 points in the deck, the opponents cannot have two aces. However, they can have an ace and a king. And when defending against a badly bid slam, opponents seem to cash those cards with revolting regularity. Blackwood simply does not fit all big hands.

Consider this case:

WEST	EAST	WEST	EAST
♠ K Q J 9 6 4	♠ A 10 7 3	1 ♠	3 ♠
♡ K Q 10	♡ A J 2	4 NT	5 ♡
◇ 7 6	◇ 8 4	?	
♣ A Q	♣ K J 10 7		

West asked his question with his 4 NT bid: "Partner, how many aces do you hold?" He got his answer when East properly bid 5 ♡, showing two aces. Then, sadly enough, West did not know what to do. Could he make six spades or not? *Which* two aces did East have? Unwilling to be accused of having no sporting blood, West bid the small slam anyway. And the defenders promptly cashed two diamond tricks.

West probably tried to find some way to blame his partner. No good. East's bidding was beyond criticism. With four trumps including two honors, thirteen high-card points and a doubleton, East's double raise in spades was correct.

Give East a slightly different hand, but with the same distribution and same high-card count:

WEST	EAST
♠ K Q J 9 6 4	♠ A 10 7 3
♡ K Q 10	♡ 4 2
◊ 7 6	◊ A J 4
♣ A Q	♣ K J 3 2

With these two hands a small slam would be easy—West would discard his second diamond on East's clubs.

The point is that West should not have used the Blackwood Convention. *It is almost always best to refrain from using the 4 NT bid, asking for aces, when you have a worthless doubleton in an unbid suit.* However, do not be discouraged. There are ways to carefully investigate slam possibilities with hands like that, and we will look into those methods later.

Now take a look at this one. You hold:

♠ K Q J 10 9 8 7 6 3 2
♡ A
◊ A
♣ 2

A little extreme perhaps, and not a hand you pick up every week or even every five years. But it does illustrate a point. Your partner is the dealer and bids 1 ♡. Let's say you bid 2 ♠ and partner rebids 3 ♡. Now you bid 4 NT. This is the ideal hand for the use of Blackwood. You are interested in absolutely nothing except the number of aces your partner holds.

In the unlikely event that he has none, you go to 5 ♠ and make the contract. If he shows one ace you bid 6 ♠. And if he shows two aces, you of course put the hand in a grand slam.

Getting back to the players who are fascinated with point count, note that you could make a grand slam on this hand if your partner had a certain specific eight points—the two black aces. This would give the partnership only 22 high-card points!

Your partner could also have:

♠ 4
♡ K Q J 8 7
◇ K Q J 2
♣ K Q J

This hand contains 18 high-card points. You would have as many as 32 points in the partnership, but you could not even make a small slam.

It comes down to this: *If the answer to your 4 NT bid will not give you the key to the slam, do not use Blackwood.*

ASKING FOR ACES

The Blackwood Slam Convention is initiated with a bid of 4 NT. This asks the simple question: Partner, how many aces do you hold? Partner responds in this manner:

Response	*Number of aces shown*
5 ♣	None or all four
5 ◇	One
5 ♡	Two
5 ♠	Three

Do not let that 5 ♣ response showing no aces or all four aces worry you. You will always be able to know which it is. For example, if you bid 4 NT with no aces in your hand, you would certainly have to hold practically all of the kings and queens. Right? Otherwise how could you sensibly be trying for a slam? Now with your hand chock-full of royalty, you bid 4 NT asking for aces and partner responds with a bid of 5 ♣. If he has no aces, how could he have bid in such a manner that you were encouraged to try for twelve tricks? In fact, how could he have made any bid at all? Undoubtedly in this situation his 5 ♣ bid shows all four aces.

Similarly, when you bid 4 NT holding one or more aces, partner's 5 ♣ response obviously shows no aces. If you have even one, partner could not have four unless it was a faulty deck.

ASKING FOR KINGS

After a bid of 4 NT and the appropriate response, the 4 NT bidder may wish to investigate grand-slam possibilities. He can ask his partner how many kings he holds by bidding 5 NT. Partner responds as follows:

Response	Number of kings shown
6 ♣	None
6 ◇	One
6 ♡	Two
6 ♠	Three
6 NT	Four

Note that in showing kings in response to partner's 5 NT bid, you bid 6 NT (not 6 clubs) to show all four kings. The reason is, since the partnership has all four aces and all four kings, there is no further reason to worry about "bidding space"—and partner will presumably bid the grand slam.

When you respond to your partner's 4 NT call, your only duty is to say how many aces you hold. At this stage only your partner knows how many aces the partnership possesses. It is not up to you to decide about a slam. If partner stops at five of your agreed suit, you should pass except in most unusual circumstances (which we will look into later).

However, if your partner follows up your 4 NT response with a bid of 5 NT, you may emerge from that menial position of letting him make all the decisions. Partner is no longer captain of the hand, for his 5 NT call not only asks you about kings, but also says that your partnership has all four aces. With that knowledge you may be justified in pushing to a grand slam. A singleton in an unbid suit or solidity in your long side suit could be the justification, after you discover that the enemy has no aces at all. In any case, when partner bids 4 NT and then 5 NT you no longer have to sit there like a dummy, meekly telling about your kings and then subsiding. You are a full partner once again.

No specific holding is required to bid 4 NT asking for aces. The previous bidding must have indicated a reasonable possibility of slam and (usually) must have located a good fit in a suit to use as the trump suit. Also, as the person who initiates the Blackwood bidding, you should feel sure that you will be safe at the five level regardless of partner's response.

THE RULE OF ONE AND TWO

In two infrequent situations you should take the following suggested precautions. (1) When you must play a hand at some number of clubs—that is, when the bidding indicates that you cannot play successfully at a major suit or at notrump—you should have two aces in your hand to initiate the Blackwood Convention with a call of 4 NT. (2) When diamonds is the only suit you can play successfully, you should have at least one ace to bid 4 NT.

Such precaution helps to avoid the awful situation where you bid 4 NT on a club hand and with only one ace and just hope partner has at least two aces. If he does have two, you are prepared to bid a small slam. But in response to your 4 NT bid partner shows only one ace, with a call of 5 ◊. Partner's previous strong bidding, including a strong raise for your clubs, was made up of kings and queens and singletons. You therefore find yourself in the rather silly position of having pushed the bidding past the only contract you can make, which is 5 ♣.

We might call this the *rule of one and two*. The rule can be violated when your partner's bidding has been so strong that you are willing to go to a small slam *without even asking for aces,* but would like to bid 4 NT to test possibilities of a grand slam. Consider this setup, for example:

WEST	EAST
♠ K Q J	♠ 2
♡ 3 2	♡ A K J 7 6 5
◇ K Q	◇ A J 7
♣ A Q 10 4 3 2	♣ K J 8

West opens the bidding with 1 ♣ and East gives an immediate jump response of 2 ♡. West bids 3 ♣ and partner raises to 4 ♣. Now West bids 4 NT even though the agreed suit is clubs and he has only one ace. The reason is that East practically *must* have two aces to justify his strong bidding. And if he has three, it may be possible to reach and make a grand slam.

SECOND- AND THIRD-ROUND CONTROLS

In many partnerships, the first partner beguiled by the sweet scent of slam barges immediately into 4 NT. This is something less than scientific. In fact, it is downright unintelligent. Information as to the number of aces held by a partnership is almost always more valuable to the partner with second- and third-round controls (kings and queens and singletons). And it is often possible to "steer" the bidding so that this player does have the opportunity to make the 4 NT call. This is an extremely important point that is well-illustrated by the following horrible example:

WEST	EAST	WEST	EAST
♠ A 9 3	♠ K Q J 10 5	1 ◇	2 ♠
♡ K 5 4	♡ A Q 6	4 NT!	5 ◇
◇ A 9 7 5 2	◇ K Q 4	6 ♣	Pass
♣ A 10	♣ K 7		

As you see, these players missed a laydown grand slam at spades or notrump. The trouble was that the opener jumped the gun in the use of the Blackwood Convention. It has already been pointed out that Blackwood should be used only when the information needed to judge the maximum contract is limited to the number of aces held by partner. West in this case got that information. He learned that his partner had one ace (which he might have guessed anyway) and he still did not know the limit of the hand. Even if he had bid 5 NT and discovered that his partner had three kings, he would not have known the extent of East's hand. Note that East could have bid just as he did if his queen of diamonds were replaced with the trey of diamonds. And in that case, six *would* be the limit of the hand.

Actually, the right contract was 7 NT, and West's second bid should have been a simple raise of his partner's spades. East could then make the 4 NT bid and follow with 5 NT at his next turn. He would find out that the opener held the aces of spades, diamonds and clubs and the king of hearts. After this lovely and logical sequence, two small children would reach the grand slam.

West's premature and haphazard action in bulling into 4 NT and then not knowing what to do is something like walking along the edge of a precipice blindfolded. But the solution is ridiculously simple. Just take off the blindfold, which in this case means letting the "right" partner utter the words "four notrump."

PLAYING AT 5 NT

When a 4 NT bidder follows his partner's ace response with a 5 NT call, he is asking about kings. Therefore the Blackwood initiator cannot stay out of a bad slam by bidding 5 NT with the intention of playing the hand there. However, it is often possible for him to require his partner to bid the correct 5 NT. He does this by naming a previously unbid suit at the five level, after getting his partner's response to the 4 NT call. For example:

WEST	EAST	WEST	EAST
♠ K Q 9	♠ 7	1 ◇	1 ♡
♡ A Q	♡ K J 10 6 5	2 NT	4 ◇
◇ K Q 9 7 3	◇ A J 10 5	4 NT	5 ◇
♣ K 10 2	♣ Q 7 3	5 ♠	5 NT
		Pass	

After West learned about his partner's big diamond fit, he was willing to try for a slam if the responder had two or more aces. When responder showed only one ace, opener knew that the idea of a slam would have to be abandoned. Therefore he bid 5 ♠, a suit not previously mentioned in the auction. This was a command to reponder to bid 5 NT and close the bidding.

This device is especially useful at match-point duplicate bridge. The score for bidding a vulnerable game at a major suit and making five would be 650. Bidding and making five notrump results in a score of 660. This modest ten-point difference could well be the difference between a poor score and a tie for top.

SHOWING VOIDS

A void suit should *not* be counted as an ace in responding to a Blackwood 4 NT bid. The principal reason is that there is too great a danger of duplication of values.

Consider this situation:

WEST	EAST	WEST	EAST
♠ K Q 8 6 4 3	♠ A J 10 2	1 ♠	3 ♠
♡ 5	♡ K 7 3 2	4 NT	5 ◇
◇ A K Q 9	◇ ——	6 ♠	Pass
♣ A 4	♣ K 9 8 3 2		

If East had treated his diamond void as the equivalent of an ace and had bid 5 ♡, West would have been completely justified in assuming that his partner had the ace of hearts and the ace of spades. West undoubtedly would then have checked on kings, and finding that his partner had two kings as well as two aces, would have bid the grand slam. The opponents would cash the ace of hearts—and another beautiful partnership would be ruined.

There is a way to show a void suit when responding to 4 NT, but you must pick your spots carefully. Bid the number of aces you hold (diamonds for one, hearts for two, etc.), but at the *six* level instead of at the five level. Remember, however, that you take this action *only* when your void is in a suit that you feel sure your partner can identify.

Consider the following hand:

	WEST	EAST
♠	K 7 6	——
♡	A Q 8 7 6 2	K J 9 4 3
◇	K Q 2	A 9 8 6
♣	A	K 7 6 4

WEST	NORTH	EAST	SOUTH
1 ♡	1 ♠	3 ♡	Pass
4 NT	Pass	6 ◇	Pass
7 ♡	Pass	Pass	Pass

When West bid 4 NT, East felt confident that a contract of 6 ♡ could be made. This is the ideal situation in which to show a void in response to a 4 NT bid—that is, *when your void is in a suit bid by the opponents*. The danger of duplication of values is practically nil, and partner can identify the suit in which you hold no cards. Even where duplication of values does exist (the case where partner has the ace of the opponents' suit and you have a void), partner will recognize the duplication and will act accordingly.

East, as we saw, was not satisfied to bid 5 ◇ in reponse to

the 4 NT call. He bid 6 ◇, showing one ace and a void. West then figured his partner for the ace of diamonds, a void in spades and good heart support. He bid the grand slam, which was a laydown.

On occasion you can feel confident that your partner can identify your void suit even though your opponents have not entered the bidding. For example:

WEST	EAST
2 ♠	3 ◇
3 ♡	3 ♠
4 NT	6 ◇

The 6 ◇ bid shows one ace and a void suit. The void cannot be in diamonds since East has bid that suit. It cannot be in hearts because we all know (we do, don't we?) that a void in a suit bid by partner is a definite liability and not an asset. Therefore, by a simple process of elimination, East's void must be in the suit that nobody bid—clubs. With this information, West can make a sound decision whether to bid seven or stop at six.

There is also a situation in which the responder to a 4 NT bid can reach a reasonable decision that his void suit is a useful one, and can go on to a slam—even after the 4 NT bidder has stopped at five of the agreed suit.

East took such action in this deal:

WEST	EAST	WEST	EAST
♠ 2	♠ K Q J 10	1 ♣	2 ♡
♡ A J 6 4	♡ K Q 10 9 7 3	4 NT	5 ◇
◇ K Q 8	◇ ——	5 ♡	6 ♡!
♣ K Q J 5 2	♣ A 10 9	Pass	

When West went to 4 NT, East had no way of knowing whether the partnership was heading for a slam in hearts, clubs or notrump. He could not afford to show his one ace and a void by responding with a bid of 6 ◊ because his partner could not possibly tell that the void was in diamonds. Therefore East contented himself with a bid of 5 ◊ to show his one ace.

However, when West then went to 5 ♡, East knew for the first time that his partner had a good fit in the heart suit, almost surely including the ace of hearts. Responder then bid 6 ♡, a bid that would not have been justified if he had not been void in diamonds. The slam was not an absolutely sure thing, but it could certainly be considered an odds-on chance since West had bid clubs and had shown good heart support.

Generally speaking, the 4 NT bidder is captain of the hand. But when the responder has a void suit that his partner does not know about, he is sometimes justified in taking over the captaincy himself. The vital test is to reach a logical and affirmative answer to the question: Is my void a useful void and not a duplication of my partner's values?

Occasionally you will run across a situation where your response to a Blackwood 4 NT bid might be passed because your response happens to be in the agreed-upon suit. Here is a typical case:

WEST	EAST	WEST	EAST
♠ 8	♠ Q 5 4	1 ◊	2 ♣
♡ K 8	♡ ——	3 ♣	4 ◊
◊ A J 10 8 3 2	◊ K Q 7 6 5 4	4 NT	6 ◊!
♣ K Q 10 4	♣ A J 7 6	Pass	

If East's hand had contained no void, his automatic response to the 4 NT bid would have been five diamonds, showing one ace. As you can see, if he had made that bid, West would certainly have passed—he would have been sure the enemy held two aces. East's actual call had to be based on courage rather than science. In this case I think I would have made the same bid East did—6 ◊. The bidding indicated that most of West's cards were in diamonds and clubs. Since East had no hearts and nobody had bid hearts, the odds favored West having some cards in that suit. Based on this reasoning, West figured to be quite short in spades. If the slam came home, your partner would compliment you on your nervy, sporting bid. If it went set, you could always say your slam call was a slip of the tongue!

WHEN OPPONENTS INTERFERE

Occasionally your right-hand opponent will make some bid at the five level over your partner's 4 NT call. No way has ever been found to put an end to this dastardly practice; unfortunately it is within the rules of the game and perfectly legal. But it is nonetheless irritating, and is often damaging to the smooth flow of bidding.

There is some difference of opinion as to the best action to be taken in this situation by the partner of the 4 NT bidder. Each answer to the problem has some merit, but I think the best and certainly the simplest procedure is as follows. Assuming that you have no reason to be ashamed of your bidding up to this point, you can show your aces by bidding one notch up for each ace you hold. For example, after an opponent's overcall of 5 ◊, a 5 ♡ bid by you would show one ace, a 5 ♠ bid would show two aces, 5 NT would show three aces and so on.

However, you are not rigidly required to show aces after an opponent overcalls your partner's 4 NT bid. For one thing, your hand may have been "diluted" by the opponents' bidding. For example, a queen that you counted two points when you picked up your hand should be discounted entirely when both opponents bid the suit in which your queen is located.

Consider this bidding sequence:

SOUTH	WEST	NORTH	EAST
1 ♠	2 ♡	3 ♠	4 ♡
4 NT	5 ♡!	?	

A pass by North would say: "Either I have no aces or the intervening bid has made it unwise, in my opinion, for me to tell you how many aces I have." A double would say: "In my

opinion, the most profitable move for us is to play this hand in 5
♡ doubled. A bid of 5 ♠ would say: "Partner, I have one ace."
For example, here are three hands North might hold:

(1)   ♠ J 6 5 4   ♡ 3 2   ◇ K Q 2   ♣ A J 4 3

With this hand, North's 3 ♠ bid was slightly sub-par.
Also he has two quick heart losers and his spade support is not
too robust. "Pass" is the suggested call.

(2)   ♠ K J 10 8   ♡ 2   ◇ A 10 9 6   ♣ K J 8 2

Here North has a maximum holding for his double raise in
spades, plus a singleton heart and fine trump support. He should
willingly show his one ace with a bid of 5 ♠.

(3)   ♠ J 8 7 5   ♡ K Q 10   ◇ K Q J 7   ♣ 10 9

This is a defensive type of hand. The hearts will probably be
of little value to partner playing a spade contract, but will be
deadly defending against the opponents' hearts. "Double" is your
best call.

IMPORTANCE OF THE QUEEN OF TRUMPS

While the Blackwood Slam Convention has proved its usefulness and is employed by most players today, I am a strong
adherent of the concept that no player should follow its precepts
rigidly and to the exclusion of common sense and good judgment. And of course this applies to the use of any artificial
bidding convention.

It bears repeating that when a player bids 4 NT and at his
next turn bids 5 NT, he is not only asking about kings but he is
also saying his side has all four aces. Now either partner, with the
proper values, can put the hand in a grand slam.

The key to many grand slams is the queen of trumps. Let's
say that you have discovered, with the use of the Blackwood

Convention, that your side has all of the aces and all of the kings and that you have identified what appears to be a nice five-opposite-four trump suit. But what about the queen of trumps? Is there a third-round trump loser? The player who bid 4 NT and 5 NT may well shy away from bidding a grand slam, holding five of the trump suit to the ace-nothing, even though his partner has given him a strong raise in the trump suit. If partner's trumps are something like K 9 8 7 or even K J 7 6, the grand slam would be a poor risk. It would depend on a 2-2 break of the opposing trumps, and the odds are as follows:

Cards Missing	Percent of Probabilities	
4	3-1	49.74%
	2-2	40.70
	4-0	9.57
6	4-2	48.45%
	3-3	35.53
	5-1	14.53
	6-0	1.49

A grand slam should be bid only when odds favor it about 3-1, so bidding one based on a 2-2 split is a *very* bad bid.

This dilemma can often be solved by the use of the Blackwood Convention *plus* a bit of good judgment by the player who holds the queen of trumps.

Examine this case:

WEST	WEST	EAST
♠ K Q 8 7	1 ◇	1 ♠
♡ K 8	4 ♠	4 NT
◇ A K Q J 10	5 ◇	5 NT
♣ 3 2	?	

West knows after this sequence that his partner has three aces (West has one ace, and the 5 NT call promised that his side has all four aces). West also knows that his partner has a hand good enough to seriously consider the possibility of a grand slam. West's "book" bid in response to the 5 NT call would be 6 ♠, showing three kings. But such slavish loyalty to the convention is not recommended. East might pass 6 ♠ if he held a spade suit such as A 10 9 3 2, or even a four-card spade suit. He has no way of knowing that West has the king *and* the queen of spades, plus an absolutely solid diamond suit. If West makes the wooden response of 6 ♠ to the 5 NT call and misses an easy grand slam, partner will be unimpressed by his statement that his bid was technically correct. East would rather be "untechnical"—and score the grand slam. Moreover, East would be justified in saying that West was not using the Blackwood Convention; he was letting it use him. Over 5 NT the right bid would be 7 ♠.

At duplicate bridge an exception can be made to the "rule" that a bid of 5 NT following a 4 NT bid by the same player says that the partnership has all of the aces. At duplicate it is important to play hands at a small slam in notrump in preference to playing them at a small slam in a suit. Occasionally it is helpful to find out how many kings your partner has in order to decide whether the small slam should be played in a suit or at notrump. However, I have made a survey on this subject over the last two years and my finding, based on the element of *frequency* of usefulness, is that it is much more valuable to have the 5 NT bid promise all of the aces.

3

The Gerber 4 ♣ Convention

♠ ♡ ◇ ♣

The Blackwood 4 NT bid does not fit every big hand. The most blatant misuse of Blackwood is the case where you bid 4 NT holding a worthless doubleton in an unbid suit. Then your partner responds showing how many aces he holds—and chances are that you still do not know whether to go to a slam.

In these and other similar situations, slam possibilities should be explored by some means other than the Blackwood Convention—namely, by the use of the Gerber Convention and by cue-bids. (We will look into the matter of cue-bids a little later.)

REGULAR USE OF GERBER

Using the Gerber Convention, 4 ♣ is the bid that asks partner how many aces he has. In response to the 4 ♣ bid, partner acts as follows:

Response	Number of aces shown
4 ◇	None or all Four
4 ♡	One
4 ♠	Two
4 NT	Three

I recommend using the Gerber 4 ♣ bid to ask for aces when partner's last bid was in notrump—*and only at such times.* This releases the 4 NT call for use as a natural bid, showing general strength and values not shown by your previous bidding, and inviting partner to go on to 6 NT if he has a maximum holding for his previous bid.

Consider this typical bidding sequence:

(a)

WEST	EAST
1 ♠	2 ◇
2 ♥	3 NT
4 NT	

In this example, East's point count is not limited, as it would have been if he had made an immediate 2 NT response over West's 1 ♠ opening, thus showing thirteen to fifteen high-card points. Instead, the spread between East's possible minimum and maximum is quite a lot more. West's 4 NT bid in this case is a natural bid, inviting the notrump slam.

Incidentally, in deciding whether to accept your slam invitation or to pass, partner should consider factors other than high-card points—the length and solidity of his own suit or suits, and the possession of honor cards in your suits.

Still referring to example (a), this is what the two hands might have been:

WEST	EAST
♠ K Q J 8 7	♠ A 4
♥ A K J 9	♥ 4 3 2
◇ 7 2	◇ Q J 10 5 4
♣ K 4	♣ A Q 8

With these cards East should pass West's 4 NT bid. East has thirteen high-card points, enough to go to 3 NT over the 2 ♥ bid, but no extra values beyond that.

However, on the same bidding sequence East's hand might have been this:

(b)

WEST	EAST	WEST	EAST
♠ K Q J 8 7	♠ 10 9	1 ♠	2 ◊
♡ A K J 9	♡ 10 8 7	2 ♡	3 NT
◊ 7 2	◊ A K Q J 6	4 NT	
♣ K 4	♣ A Q 8		

In this hand East has sixteen high-card points, a solid diamond suit, mildly important intermediate cards in West's two suits and full control of the suit that nobody has bid, clubs. East should unhesitatingly go to 6 NT.

In example (b) the 4 NT call is again a natural bid. It makes West's seventeen to nineteen points easy to handle. West has both majors, but partner may be slightly below par in high-card points and there is no sense in punishing him by leaping wildly into a slam and hoping for the best. If East has bid his hand to the hilt with his 3 NT call, he can pass 4 NT. If he has hitherto undisclosed values, he can go on to slam. Leave some of the judgment features up to partner. If he consistently makes the wrong decisions, that does not mean you need a new bidding system. You need a new partner!

Remember that Gerber (the 4 ♣ bid) is *only* ace-asking *when partner's last bid was in some number of notrump.* This is especially valuable at match-point duplicate where every hand is (or should be) bid to the hilt. When you use Gerber and find that partner has one ace less than you had hoped, you can sign off at the four level—one notch lower than if you had used Blackwood. Yes, there are hands where you feel sure you are safe at the five level but go set a trick owing to some ridiculous distribution of the opposing cards.

After using the Gerber 4 ♣ Convention in the manner described, I recommend going back to Blackwood if you want to ask for kings—that is, bid 4 ♣ to ask about aces and then bid 5 NT (*not* 5 ♣) to ask about kings. Some theorists argue that this wastes much bidding space. But who cares about bidding space at the five level when you are obviously testing for a grand slam? Using 5 ♣ as Gerber, asking for kings, prevents you from ever playing a contract of 5 ♣. And in some hands that is the only contract you can make.

Here is a sequence where using 5 ♣ as a Gerber bid to ask for kings could end in disaster:

WEST	EAST
1 NT	3 ♣ (strong)
3 NT	4 ♣
4 ♡	5 ♣
Pass	

East, we may assume, has a good club suit, a good hand and slam aspirations. His 4 ♣ call was Gerber (because his partner's last bid was in notrump). West dutifully showed one ace by bidding 4 ♡. East had hoped his partner had two aces. He now gives up on the idea of a slam and puts the hand in 5 ♣, the only suit that he can play with success. Opener passes since the 5 ♣ call is a natural bid and not asking for kings.

Now to go rather far out on a limb, I recommend that a 4 ♣ bid ask for aces when partner's last bid was in notrump, *even when one or both partners have bid clubs during the auction.* Rumbles of discontent will undoubtedly emerge over this statement, but the simplicity of this method outweighs the theoretical disadvantages. Hands can be manufactured to show that mix-ups and misunderstandings can occur. But mythical hands can be devised to prove or disprove the value of any bidding device. Keeping a convention simple and easy to remember is the true measure of its effectiveness. You run into the mix-ups and misunderstandings when you add a lot of variations and exceptions. Following the principle of *always* having 4 ♣ ask for aces when partner's last bid was in notrump has served me well. And the record I have kept on the subject for several years shows not even one bad result.

Consider this deal:

WEST	EAST
♠ K J 10	♠ Q 4
♡ Q J 10	♡ K 5
◇ K Q 10 2	◇ A 5 4
♣ A 8 2	♣ K Q J 6 5 4

When West opens the bidding with 1 NT, East is entitled to consider the possibility of a slam. In fact, if West has just the right hand, including at least two aces, there *will* be a slam. For example, West could have:

♠ K 5 2   ♡ A 9 4   ◇ K Q 3 2   ♣ A 10 8

and you could win six clubs, three diamonds, two hearts and one spade.

In the actual hand shown above, West opens the bidding with 1 NT and East says 3 ♣. West rebids 3 NT and East responds with 4 ♣. This last bid is Gerber, asking for aces. Unfortunately West bids four hearts, showing only one ace. (He might have had two or even three.) East now gives up on the idea of a slam and bids 4 NT. Partner must pass, and the hand is played there. East's hand, with high cards in every suit, is well-suited to notrump play, and there is no reason to insist on a club contract. For one thing, 5 ♣ is a notch higher and therefore harder to make. For another, it does not count as much as a notrump contract.

However, in a situation like the following, different tactics would be used:

WEST   EAST
♠ K Q J 9   ♠ 2
♡ A 4 3 2   ♡ 5
◇ Q 9 5   ◇ K J 10 6
♣ A 8   ♣ K Q J 10 6 5 4

Again West opens the bidding with 1 NT. East responds 3 ♣ and West rebids 3 NT. East now bids 4 ♣, a Gerber bid asking for aces. If partner had exactly the right sixteen points there would be an excellent play for a grand slam. However, for some reason still unexplained, partner never seems to have that perfect hand. Here he could have had:

♠ A 10 9 8   ♡ A 9 8 7   ◇ A 8   ♣ A 9 8

If East could ruff out the queen of diamonds or guess where it was, he could win all thirteen tricks.

But with the actual hand West bids 4 ♠ over 4 ♣, showing only two aces and making it clear that the opponents have two. Again East gives up on the idea of a slam, but this time his hand is unsuited to notrump play. The partnership will do better to stay under the protection of East's club suit. If West played in 4 NT, a heart opening would make a shambles out of the contract. But 5 ♣ can easily be made, losing only a spade and a diamond. As you can see, if the partnership used 5 ♣ as a king-asking bid, they would not be able to stop at the 5 ♣ level. Therefore 5 NT is a better bid for asking for kings after bidding Gerber (4 ♣) for aces.

GERBER IN UNUSUAL SITUATIONS

When the early rounds of the auction include one or more bids that are completely artificial, the incipient Gerber 4 ♣ bidder must be careful to think back to his partner's last "true" bid.

For example, when the bidding has gone:

WEST	EAST
1 ♡	2 ♠
3 ◇	3 ♠
3 NT	4 ♣

East's 4 ♣ bid is clearly Gerber, asking for aces, because West's last bid was in notrump.

However, in this sequence:

WEST	EAST
1 NT	2 ♣
2 ◇	4 ♣

East's 4 ♣ call is also Gerber—because the last *natural* bid was notrump. (East's 2 ♣ bid was the Stayman Convention asking for a four-card major suit. The 2 ◊ response was also artificial, denying four cards in either major.) Thus West's next move is to answer this legitimate Gerber request for aces.

The Stayman sequence is used in the above example merely to show how artificial bids enter into the auction. The same principle applies where other conventional calls appear and where the bidding sequence might get even more complicated. The player who is considering asking about his partner's aces must plow back through the maze of artificial bids to find his partner's last true, natural bid. If that bid was in notrump, then the way to ask for aces would be Gerber. If it was a suit bid, you would use the Blackwood 4 NT.

4

Cue-bidding for Slams

♠ ♡ ◇ ♣

The Blackwood 4 NT Convention and the Gerber Convention will serve you satisfactorily in a good percentage of slam-testing situations. But there are many other hands where you need to know more about your partner's holding than merely the number of aces that were dealt to him. You may need to know *which* aces he holds, and possibly which kings and which singletons. This information can usually be shown by means of cue-bids.

The basic cue-bid situation arises after a partnership has decided on a trump suit—that is, when one partner has raised a suit bid by the other partner. Subsequent bids in other suits by either partner are cue-bids, showing controls in the form of aces, kings and singletons.

Take the situation in which you hold:

♠ A Q 10 4 3 2   ♡ 2   ◇ K Q   ♣ A Q J 9

You open the bidding with 1 ♠ and partner makes the pleasant-sounding call of 3 ♠. Looking again at your hand, you decide there is an excellent chance for slam and bid 4 NT—because you need to know only how many aces partner holds, not which aces. If partner bids 5 ◇, showing one ace, you bid 6 ♠, which will be a laydown or at the very worst will require one successful finesse.

Change your hand a trifle:

♠ A Q 10 4 3 2   ♡ 3 2   ◇ K Q   ♣ A Q J

Again you open 1 ♠ and partner raises to 3 ♠. This is an entirely different problem. If you now bid 4 NT and partner bids 5 ◇, showing one ace, you will not know whether to bid 6 ♠ or to stop at 5 ♠. Partner could have:

♠ K J 8 7   ♡ Q 6 5   ◇ A J 10 9   ♣ K 2

in which case the opponents could defeat the spade slam by cashing two fast heart tricks.

Partner might also have a hand with slightly less high-card strength but the following distribution:

♠ K J 8 7   ♡ A K 10 8 4   ◇ J 9 8   ♣ 2

With this holding opposite your hand it would take a miracle to beat six spades.

If your hand has the worthless doubleton in hearts:

♠ A Q 10 4 3 2   ♡ 3 2   ◇ K Q   ♣ A Q J

your best bet after getting a double spade raise from partner is to make the cue-bid of 4 ♣. This shows club control and also is evidence of your interest in reaching a slam. If partner, in turn, makes a cue-bid of 4 ◇, you will assume that he has the ace of that suit. But you will be able to do no more than return to 4 ♠. If partner happens to have the ace of hearts, too, he may go on to six anyway. But that is his business. You have done all you can.

If, over your 4 ♣ cue-bid, partner cue-bids hearts, you could reasonably bid 6 ♠ because the danger of the opponents winning the first two tricks in hearts is gone. You may not make six spades, but you should have a good play for it.

SEQUENCE OF CUE-BIDS

In the early days of cue-bidding, and as these bids are used by most players today, a cue-bid shows first-round control of a suit (the ace or a void). If a player has two suits that he wants to cue-bid, he always cue-bids the lower-ranking suit first.

For example, you bid 1 ♠ and partner raises that suit. Let us say you have the ace of clubs and a void in diamonds. Under present methods you would cue-bid clubs first because that is the lower-ranking suit. This may normally be the best procedure, but in certain circumstances it may not be best.

It is better to take a more realistic and practical view of cue-bidding techniques. In certain cases, which will be outlined in more detail later, the first cue-bid made in a partnership can show second-round control of a suit. Do not hold rigidly to the concept that with two cue-bids to make, you always cue-bid the lower-ranking suit first. Instead, make the cue-bid that has the best chance of clarifying your problem of deciding about a slam.

CUE-BIDDING TO SHOW SECOND-ROUND CONTROL

Early rounds of bidding may indicate that game will be reached, as in these sequences:

WEST	EAST
1 ♠	3 ♠

or

1 ♠	2 ◊
2 ♡	3 ♠

In such cases a cue-bid may be a serious try to reach a small slam. The first cue-bid made by either partner may show a second-round control (a king or a singleton). Subsequent cue-bids by either partner must, of course, show first-round control (an ace or a void).

When the early rounds of bidding indicate that a small slam will probably be reached, then a cue-bid by either partner may be construed as a serious attempt to reach a grand slam. In this case all cue-bids must show first-round controls.

For example, when the bidding proceeds:

WEST	EAST
1 ♡	2 ♠
3 ♠	

it is seldom that a partnership fails to reach a small slam. Thus all cue-bids after this type of strong sequence must show first-round controls.

Consider this hand in which quite a few pairs in a duplicate game failed to reach an easy contract of 6 ♠:

WEST	EAST	WEST	EAST
♠ A 9 5 3 2	♠ K 8 7 6	1 ♠	3 ♠
♡ A K Q 2	♡ 5 4	4 ♣	4 ◇
◇ 3 2	◇ A J 5 4	6 ♠	Pass
♣ K Q	♣ A 3 2		

The West player made seven when the opposing spades split 2-2. He discarded his second diamond on dummy's ace of clubs. Of course, seven could not be bid as the odds were sharply against finding the outstanding spades divided evenly. However, a number of pairs did not reach the 6 ♠ contract because West cue-bid 4 ♡ over his partner's 3 ♠ bid, holding doggedly to the idea that *all* cue-bids must show first-round controls. West never got the diamond cue-bid from his partner and therefore could not be sure that the opponents would not be able to cash two diamond tricks against a spade slam.

The first cue-bid you make does not have to be the "cheapest" ace (or void). From a practical and sensible standpoint, it should be the cue-bid that is most likely to get you the information you want and need to decide about a slam.

However, once your partner has made a cue-bid, you should nearly always choose the "cheapest" of your cue-bids when you have a choice. He may have chosen his bid just to see whether he could hear from you concerning the next highest ranking suit.

Here is another hand in which the use of the old-fashioned "book" methods would probably fail to reach a contract of 6 ♠:

WEST	EAST	WEST	EAST
♠ A Q 10 5 4	♠ K 9 8 6	1 ♠	3 ♠
♡ 5 4	♡ A 9	4 ◊	4 ♡
◊ K Q 10	◊ A J 8 7	6 ♠	Pass
♣ A K 2	♣ 7 6 4		

West elected not to use the 4 NT bid for his second call—if he had gotten a 5 ◊ response showing one ace, he would not know which ace it was and there would be the danger of two quick heart losers. East's hand might be:

♠ K J 9 8   ♡ Q J 6   ◊ A J 9 8 7   ♣ 3

West chose to cue-bid his second-round control in diamonds rather than his first-round control in clubs because it would be easy and logical for his partner to cue-bid the ace of hearts, if he had it. If East did not bid 4 ♡ over the 4 ◊ call, West planned to stop at 4 ♠. However, West did get the 4 ♡ bid he was hoping for, and the spade slam was a laydown.

Now let's look at the bidding if the cue-bids were made "by the book"—lower-ranking suit first:

WEST	EAST
1 ♠	3 ♠
4 ♣	4 ◊
4 ♠	Pass

Over the 4 ♣ bid East dutifully cue-bid his ace of diamonds. West then went to four spades, fearful of two quick heart

losers. It was difficult now for East to take further action as there
were no extra values above his first bid of 3 ♠.

Here is another example:

WEST	EAST	WEST	EAST
♠ A J 10 9 4 3	♠ K Q 8 7	1 ♠	3 ♠
♡ A K Q J	♡ 5 4	4 ♣	4 ♠
◊ 5 2	◊ Q J 9 4	Pass	
♣ 3	♣ A J 9		

In this deal a cue-bid of either 4 ♣ or 4 ♡ by West would
get the partnership in the right spot—4 ♠.

But let's change East's hand slightly. We will give him the
same 4-4-3-2 distribution and the same high-card count (13
points). But interchange his diamonds and clubs so that his hand
will be:

♠ K Q 8 7   ♡ 5 4   ◊ A J 9   ♣ Q J 9 4

Now if West cue-bids hearts at his second turn, East can do
no more than return to 4 ♠, thus missing a slam. But if West
makes the recommended second-round control cue-bid of 4 ♣, it
is easy and natural for East to make the cue-bid of 4 ◊. This is
the beautiful sound that West wanted to hear so that he could bid
the spade slam, making it by discarding dummy's jack and nine
of diamonds on his hearts and then ruffing his second diamond in
dummy.

Some of the close slams missed by half the field in a duplicate game can be reached more easily with the type of cue-bid
that gives partner the best chance to cooperate.

Take this one, for example:

WEST	EAST (hand 1)	EAST (hand 2)
♠ A 9 7 6 5	♠ K 8 4 2	♠ K 8 4 2
♡ 6 5	♡ K Q 8	♡ A J 9
◊ K Q 4	◊ A J 10 2	◊ A J 10 2
♣ A K Q	♣ 5 4	♣ 5 4

The bidding:

WEST	EAST
1 ♠	3 ♠
4 ♣	4 ◇
4 ♠	Pass

With the first East hand, the right contract of 4 ♠ would be reached whether West cue-bid diamonds or clubs at his second turn. A slam would be a bad risk as it would depend on a 2-2 split of the opposing spades, which is much less than a 50-50 shot.

On the second East hand, however, if West cue-bid clubs at his second turn, East would say 4 ◇ as before and West would still be in doubt about the heart situation. If West cue-bids 4 ◇, East will cue-bid the ace of hearts, taking the curse off that suit and enabling West to take a shot at the slam. (This is a close one and he might not make it, but the odds in his favor would be over 50 percent. He would have two chances—a 2-2 spade break or, if the spades break 3-1, finding the opponent with the three spades also holding at least three diamonds. In this latter case he could pitch his heart loser on the fourth round of diamonds as the opponent ruffed with the high trump. And of course, without a heart opening lead he would have plenty of time. Assuming no worse than a 3-1 trump break, he could give up a spade while dummy still had the ace of hearts and again pitch his second heart on dummy's fourth diamond.)

You do not get an overwhelming score for bidding slams that are so obvious that everybody in the room reaches them. The close ones get you the tie-for-top scores.

In the West hand just discussed, West had a choice between cue-bidding a suit in which he had second-round control and one in which he had first-round control. He chose the second-round control and it worked well in connection with the second East hand. However, there is no intention of recommending this choice as a consistent pattern of bidding. There is no magic advantage in showing a second-round control ahead of a first-round control. The first player to cue-bid should simply make the choice that is most likely to get him the specific information he is seeking in order to make a reasonable decision about a slam.

In the following hand, West chose to cue-bid his cheapest control, which happened to be an ace, because this action would give his partner every possible opportunity to clarify his holding.

WEST	EAST	WEST	EAST
♠ A K 6 5 4 3	♠ Q J 9 2	1 ♠	3 ♠
♡ K Q 2	♡ A 7 6	4 ♣	4 ♡
◊ ——	◊ K J 8 4	5 ♡	6 ♣
♣ A Q 4 2	♣ K 9	7 ♠	Pass

West had a big hand, and his aspirations were of the grand-slam variety. However, the Blackwood 4 NT Convention did not fit the situation. If West bid 4 NT and found that his partner had one ace, he would not know which red ace it was. If it were the diamond ace, the opponents would have a live ace of hearts and the grand slam would be impossible.

So West used the cue-bid of 4 ♣. It was good news when East bid 4 ♡. By negative inference it was now clear that East did not have the ace of diamonds and that the awful duplication of an ace opposite a void did not exist. It was East's duty to show his cheapest first-round control over the 4 ♣ call, and therefore his failure to bid 4 ◊ denied that he held the ace of that suit.

But the road to the grand slam was not yet completely clear. West knew East had approximately 13 high-card points, as promised by his jump raise in spades. But these points could include the king, queen and jack of diamonds and he could have two low clubs.

West bided his time with a cue-bid of 5 ♡, indicating second-round control of that suit. This left the way open for East to bid 6 ♣, which showed second-round club control. This could be the king of clubs or it could be a singleton. Either way, West was justified in bidding the grand slam, which could be soundly reached in no other way than by the use of this excellent series of cue-bids.

CUE-BIDDING TO REACH 3 NT

Cue-bids are most useful in reaching slams, but they are also of outstanding usefulness in the lower ranges of bidding. In particular, they are a great help in getting a partnership to three notrump in the case where each partner is wide open in some suit. Consider the following case, for example:

WEST	EAST
♠ 4 3	♠ A 10 2
♡ A Q 9	♡ 8 6
◇ K Q 8 7 4	◇ A J 9 6 5
♣ A 9 2	♣ K 8 3

Let's say that West opens the bidding with 1 ◇ and East raises to 3 ◇. If it were not for cue-bids, West would now be in a bit of difficulty. His hand is well over a minimum and his partner has given him a jump raise. Should he go on to game at diamonds? There should be some play for that contract, although on the actual cards it would go set if the king of hearts was wrong.

West could hardly be expected to say 3 NT with the small doubleton in an unbid suit (spades). But the solution is simple. West bids 3 ♡, stating that he has hearts stopped and, by inference, asking his partner if he is interested in a notrump game. East could have bid 3 NT here, with both spades and clubs stopped. Actually, he elected to bid 3 ♠, saying that he had that suit stopped. Possibly he thought it would be better to have the opening lead come up to West's hand. Anyway, this took the curse off the spade suit and West bid 3 NT, which was a lay-down.

There is very little chance of misunderstandings in sequences of this kind. If East did not know immediately whether his partner's 3 ♡ bid was a slam try or merely an attempt to reach 3 NT, it would not make any difference. If he dutifully bid 3 ♠ to show that he had that suit stopped, the situation would be clarified for him by his partner's next bid.

These tactics also come into play when an opponent gets into the bidding, as in this setup:

NORTH
♠ A K 10 8
♡ 4 3 2
◇ J 5 3
♣ A 8 6

SOUTH
♠ 6 5
♡ A 10 7
◇ A K Q 10 2
♣ Q 4 2

The bidding:

SOUTH (dealer)	WEST	NORTH	EAST
1 ◇	Pass	1 ♠	2 ♣
2 ◇	Pass	3 ♣	Pass
3 NT	Pass	Pass	Pass

Here again we have the situation where 3 NT is cold. But it is difficult to reach because South is afraid of clubs and North is afraid of hearts. South could have passed over East's 2 ♣ bid, but as he was well over a minimum in high cards and had a good solid diamond suit, his free rebid was fully justified. North had no distributional advantages but he had good high cards (about the equal of an opening bid), plus a mild ability to play diamonds. There was no risk, then, in trying for game at notrump. North's 3 ♣ cue-bid said he had the opponent's clubs stopped. With this knowledge South bid 3 NT, and nine tricks were readily available. (Five diamonds might have made, but probably not if the defenders attacked hearts immediately.)

It should be remembered that cue-bids of the types just illustrated are not *commands* for partner to bid 3 NT. *Cue-bids are merely suggestions or invitations.* Partner does not have to bid 3 NT. In fact, he should not do so unless, with the information you have given him plus his own cards, he knows that all suits are stopped. He should also know that he will have a good play for a total of nine tricks.

In the cue-bids we have just looked at, a player who bid a certain suit was saying that he had it stopped. Some players handle cue-bids the other way around. That is, when they make a cue-bid of this sort they are not telling partner they have the suit stopped, but they are asking partner if *he* has it stopped. There are advantages to both methods, and you can take your choice. I just happen to prefer cue-bids the way they are illustrated here.

FIVE-LEVEL ASKING BIDS

Occasionally you will encounter a hand that does not seem to fit Blackwood, Gerber or cue-bids. Suppose you held this hand:

♠ K J 6
♡ 3 2
◇ A K Q J 9
♣ A 3 2

Your partner is the dealer and bids 1 ♠. You consider whether to make a jump shift of 3 ◇ or to bid only 2 ◇. The heart suit bothers you, and you decide you can obtain more information about it without crowding the bidding by using a series of forcing bids. Thus you decide to bid only 2 ◇. Your partner rebids 2 ♠.

What is your next bid? We immediately toss out 3 ◇—partner could pass that. A bid of 4 ♠ is not enough with your fine hand, which includes good spade support. And 6 ♠ is too much and may well go set. A bid of 5 ♠ is a cloudy decision and would undoubtedly result in confusing partner—he would not know exactly what you are driving at or what you expect him to have in order to go on to a small slam.

Well, let's look at both hands:

WEST	EAST	WEST	EAST
♠ K J 6	♠ A Q 10 9 5 4		1 ♠
♡ 3 2	♡ Q 5 4	2 ◊	2 ♠
◊ A K Q J 9	◊ 7	3 ♣	3 ♠
♣ A 3 2	♣ K J 10	5 ♠	Pass

West's 3 ♣ call is the key bid. That bid was not made to be
fancy, but merely to get it into the history of the bidding. The
partnership has now bid three suits, and West's following jump to
5 ♠ should make his intentions crystal-clear. The message of the
5 ♠ bid is: "Partner, we have bid three suits and I have leaped to
five of a major. This would be an absurd call, taken by itself, as
there is no bonus for bidding and making five. If we stopped at
four and made five, we would get the same score. Therefore, I
must be guaranteeing five-odd and also trying for a slam. I am
ordering you to bid six spades if you do not have two quick losers
in the suit nobody bid—hearts."

This is a rather long-winded message and partner would
probably go to sleep if you read it to him out of this book. But if
he is any kind of a partner at all, it will take him only a second or
two to bid 6 ♠ if he has the ace, the king or a singleton in the
heart suit.

In the actual hand, East would pass 5 ♠ since he does have
two quick heart losers. However, change his king of clubs to the
king of hearts and he should unhesitatingly go to the small slam
in spades. If the opponents take their ace of hearts at trick one,
East-West will have the next twelve tricks. If they do not, there is
still an excellent chance for the slam. The opposing diamonds
could split 4-3 or the ten of diamonds could drop; and if neither
of these things happen, declarer could always fall back on the
good fortune of finding the ace of hearts in front of the king.

BLACKWOOD AFTER CUE-BIDDING

Sometimes the Blackwood Convention is used after a series
of cue-bids. Since a first-round control may consist of a void suit
on occasion, it is not wise to count the ace of such a cue-bid in
responding to the Blackwood Convention. This is only true,

however, where the cue-bid positively guaranteed first-round control. If the cue-bid could have been second-round control, any ace in that suit should be shown in response to the Blackwood Convention.

Each partnership should have a positive understanding as to what cue-bids positively guarantee first-round controls and what cue-bids could be second-round controls. Here is what I recommend:

(1)   After a suit is agreed upon, the first cue-bid is *not* guaranteed to be a first-round control.

(2)   A cue-bid in a suit previously bid *by your partner* is not necessarily a first-round control. It could be first-round or second-round control.

(3)   All subsequent cue-bids are positively first-round controls.

(4)   All cue-bids of new suits show positive first-round control in a sequence where a former bid has virtually assured a small slam and the only question is whether a grand slam should be bid.

As we saw in a previous chapter, the first player to make a cue-bid may make that bid in a suit that will secure him the greatest amount of information, and need not necessarily make it the cheapest cue-bid available. However, if his partner chooses to respond with a cue-bid, he should nearly always choose the cheapest possible cue-bid.

Here is the way it might work out in practice:

WEST	EAST
1 ♣	1 ◊
1 ♠	3 ♠ (1)
4 ♣ (2)	4 ◊ (3)
4 ♡ (4)	4 ♠ (5)
4 NT (6)	5 ♣ (7)
6 ♠ (8)	

(1) Setting the suit.

(2) A cue-bid. Starting slam investigation. This is not necessarily a first-round control, although in this case, West does happen to have first-round control. This is the first cue-bid in a series and is not a suit previously bid by *partner*.

(3) This bid definitely guarantees first-round control of diamonds. It is not the first cue-bid in the series, nor is it a suit previously bid by *partner*.

(4) This is a definitely first-round control, as it is not the first cue-bid in the series nor is it a suit previously bid by *partner*.

(5) East has no additional values to show.

(6) This says how many aces do you have outside of those suits where first-round control has been definitely shown?

(7) First-round control has already been shown in hearts and diamonds. Outside of these two suits, I have no aces at all.

(8) Six spades is the limit of the hand.

The hands might be:

WEST	EAST
♠—K Q 9 6 4	♠—J 10 8 5
♡—	♡—A Q 6
◇—K 4	◇—A 10 5 3
♣—A K Q 9 4 2	♣—10 7

By this sequence of bidding, West learned that the ace of spades was missing. East might have held:

♠—A 10 8 5   ♡—Q J 6   ◇—A 10 5 3   ♣—10 7

Had East held this hand, his response to the 4 NT bid would have been 5 ◇ saying I hold one ace outside of the red suits. West would then have bid a grand slam knowing that his partner held the ace of spades and the ace of diamonds.

5

When Is Blackwood Blackwood?

♠ ♡ ◇ ♣

This silly-looking sentence would make no sense at all to a non-bridge player, but readers of this book will certainly understand it. While it is consoling to know that in a very large percentage of cases the partner of a 4 NT bidder will know whether or not the 4 NT call is asking for aces, it must be admitted that there are situations where there can be a little doubt. And this applies even in the case of experienced partnerships. We will try to clarify these "fringe" situations.

First, let me say that when I originated the Blackwood Slam Convention more than thirty years ago, the bidding structure was relatively simple—at least as compared with the complexities of today's game. Developments since that time have made it necessary to make some changes in the convention. This is not because there were any inherent faults in the convention as originally devised. Rather, the 4 NT bid can now be more effective and useful in certain situations if it means something other than "Partner, how many aces do you hold?"

The two principal conventions that have made changes in the original Blackwood desirable are John Gerber's 4 ♣ Convention, asking for aces, and the unusual notrump convention originated by Alvin Roth and Tobias Stone.

The first and most obviously desirable change in the original Blackwood Convention was to use 5 ♣ in response to partner's 4 NT call to show either all four aces or none, instead of using a response of 5 NT to show all four aces. This enabled the 4 NT bidder to continue with the king-asking bid (5 NT) on those rare occasions when he bid 4 NT without any aces at all and found his partner holding all four of them.

In the early days of the Blackwood Convention it was recommended that a bid of 4 NT followed up by a bid of 5 NT by the same player guaranteed that the partnership held all four aces *at rubber bridge,* but *not at duplicate.* The idea was, of course, that even when the opponents held one ace it would still be profitable to check on kings and see if the hand could be played at the higher-paying 6 NT spot rather than at six of a suit.

Based on the simple standard of frequency of usefulness, this practice has been abandoned. Now, if you bid 4 NT and then 5 NT you are guaranteeing that your side has all the aces, whether you are playing duplicate or rubber bridge. Thus either partner may put the hand in a grand slam if he has the values that seem to justify such action. The knowledge that the partnership has all four aces is usually the vital point in reaching a successful grand slam in this manner.

4 NT AS A NOTRUMP RAISE

As discussed earlier, my version of the Gerber Convention is that if my partner's last true bid was notrump, then a bid of four notrump by me is simply a notrump raise suggesting a notrump slam. If my partner had a maximum holding for his previous bid, he can bid 6 NT. If his holding was minimum or near-minimum, he can pass and play 4 NT. A bid of 4 ♣ over my partner's last true notrump call is Gerber, asking for aces.

Recommending, as always, that you should leave a little judgment in the game instead of holding rigidly to *any* convention, the following bidding sequence would be an exception:

WEST	EAST
1 ♡	2 ♠
2 NT	3 ◇
3 NT	4 ◇
4 NT	

It would be absurd for East to consider his partner's 4 NT bid as Blackwood, asking for aces and trying for a slam. West's first rebid was the weakest call he could make, showing no interest in spades and inability to rebid hearts. His 3 NT bid was also the weakest call he could make, this time showing no interest in either spades or diamonds, and certainly announcing that he had an absolutely minimum opening bid.

West could construe East's 4 ◊ bid either as one last slam try or as evidence that East did not think he could stand playing in notrump. Actually it would make no difference how he construed it, and West's bid of 4 NT should clearly show that he desperately wishes to play at that contract and not get any higher. He probably has not more than two spades and either two or three diamonds and something like A J 10 or some other two-stopper holding in the unbid suit, clubs.

Since 4 ♣ asks for aces only when partner's last bid was in notrump, there does not need to be any confusion when one partner, or even both partners, have bid clubs during the auction. Consider the following sequence:

WEST	EAST
1 ♣	1 ♡
1 ♠	3 ♣
3 ♡	3 NT
4 ♣	4 ♡
?	

West's 4 ♣ bid was Gerber because his partner's last bid was in notrump. East so read it and bid 4 ♡ to indicate possession of one ace. West now had all roads open to him. If the response to his 4 ♣ bid told him that his opponents held two aces, he could bid 5 ♣ and play it there. If he wished to play 4 NT, he could bid that and East would pass and play it there. If he had located all of the aces, he could, if he wished, bid 5 NT to ask his partner about kings.

4 NT AS THE UNUSUAL NOTRUMP

There are also times when it will be more profitable to use 4 NT as the unusual notrump rather than as a Blackwood call asking for aces. The unusual notrump convention has variations, but basically it is similar to a takeout double, asking partner to bid his best minor suit. It must be used only when it is perfectly clear to partner that you cannot want to play at notrump.

To take an extreme example, suppose you are the dealer and pass, indicating that you cannot even muster up thirteen points. Both opponents show strength by bidding, your partner passes and at your next turn you say 2 NT or 3 NT or even 4 NT. A small child would know that you are certainly not serious about wanting to play notrump. Assuming that your opponents have bid spades and hearts, your partner will take your notrump call as unusual and will bid his best minor suit.

Most frequently the unusual-notrump bidder will have a hand of somewhat limited high-card strength. But he will have (or should have) excellent distribution, including at least five cards in each minor suit. The bid is most often used as a sacrifice or attempt thereat. For example, your opponents are vulnerable (you are not). By strong bidding they reach a contract of 4 ♠. You hold:

♠ 2   ♡ 2   ◇ A J 9 7 6 5   ♣ K Q 10 8 3

You feel that you have little chance to defeat their contract and that they could not beat you too badly if you were to play five of a minor. Your bid of 4 NT here would be clearly unusual, and your partner should bid his best minor. If you simply bid five in your longer minor (diamonds) partner might put down a hand with the singleton deuce of diamonds and four clubs to the jack. Obviously it is much more sensible to tell partner you can play either minor, then let him look in his hand and make the decision.

Every new artificial-bidding convention is subject to abuse and mishandling by a great number of players, and this is also true of the unusual notrump. Most of the mishandling is done by players who look upon each new convention as a sort of magic formula that will lead them out of the wilderness of below-average scores. Eagerness to capitalize on the supposed advantages of the unusual notrump convention impels such players to use it when they hold only four cards in each minor suit or when they have overlooked some clue in the opponents' bidding that indicates that their partner figures to be short in both minors.

For example, suppose East and West have bid like this:

WEST	EAST
1 ♠	2 ♡
2 ♠	3 ♡
Pass	

If this bidding comes around to North, there is clear evidence that the opponents have a misfit. East has hearts—probably six of them—but chances are that he has a singleton spade. Therefore he is long in at least one of the minors. By the same reasoning, West is long in spades but very short in hearts, and thus probably long in one of the minors. If North has, say, nine cards in the minor suits, there is an excellent chance that his partner has something like three cards in one minor and two in the other—or worse.

On the other hand, on bidding like this from the opponents:

WEST	EAST
1 ♠	2 ♡
3 ♡	3 ♠
4 ♠	

North's use of the unusual notrump convention is much more likely to get a good result. On the bidding, both of the opponents could well have nine cards in the major suits, and therefore are likely to be short in both minors. South, then, figures to have some decent length in at least one of the minors. Of course, it should be assumed that if North does go for the sacrifice contract by bidding 4 NT over the opponents' 4 ♠, he has practically no prospects of defeating their contract.

We have discussed the unusual notrump as a type of takeout double asking partner to bid his best minor suit. Many players extend its use to request partner to bid his best of the unbid suits. This usage occurs when the opponents have bid one major and one minor, as where they open the bidding with 1 ◊ and later reach a contract of 4 ♠. If you elect to say 4 NT over the 4 ♠ bid, it is not Blackwood. (You could hardly be trying for a slam when your side has not even entered the auction previously.) This 1 NT call is the unusual notrump requesting partner to bid at the five level in clubs or hearts, whichever is his better suit.

Occasionally (and you should hope it *never* occurs) an opponent will open the bidding with a high preemptive bid, depriving you of the opportunity of exchanging valuable information with your partner at the lower levels. There is no absolute perfect way to deal with this situation, and you simply have to do the best you can. Consider this unusual situation:

EAST (not vulnerable)   SOUTH (vulnerable)
4 ♠   4 NT

South's 4 NT bid should not be considered as Blackwood. It is a request to North to bid his best of the three remaining suits. It is undeniably true that hands can be manufactured where South would *want* his 4 NT bid to be Blackwood, asking for aces. For example, he could hold this almost perfect hand:

♠ ——   ♡ K Q J 10 9 8 3   ◊ A K Q   ♣ K Q J

If North showed one ace South could bid 6 ♡. However, it might turn out that North's one ace was the ace of spades, in which case the slam would be set. If North showed two aces, South still would not know whether to bid 6 ♡ or 7 ♡.

However, South's 4 NT call over East's 4 ♠ preempt should be construed as a request for North to bid his best of the other three suits. The recommendation is made on the same basis as previous recommendations in this book—frequency of usefulness.

Here is another situation that looks about the same as the last one but actually is quite different:

EAST	SOUTH
4 ♡	4 NT

In this case the spade suit is open. That is, nobody has bid it. South's 4 NT bid is not Blackwood and it also is not a request that his partner bid *any* one of the other three suits. If South were interested in spades *he* could have bid 4 ♠. Or he might have doubled, which would show some support for spades and leave a little of the judgment factor up to his partner. North could then bid 4 ♠ if he had a decent holding, or leave the double in if he thought that would be the best action.

In any case, it would not make much sense for South to be asking his partner to bid spades at the five level. Based on this reasoning, and again applying the principle of frequency of usefulness, South's 4 NT should be construed as asking North to bid his best *minor* suit.

Now, to get into even muddier waters, consider this use of the 4 NT bid:

EAST	SOUTH
4 ♣ *or* 4 ♢	4 NT

I have never seen this particular sequence come up in actual play, but of course it could. This 4 NT bid should not be considered as a request for partner to bid any suit at the five level—a cue-bid of 5 ♣ would be available for that purpose. This leaves the choice between Blackwood and a desire to play the hand at the contract of 4 NT. On the basis of frequency, Blackwood wins, but only by a nose. The best advice on the handling of these fringe situations is to talk them over with your favorite partners and come to a conclusion as to exactly how you are going to handle them. And of course this information should be willingly imparted to your opponents.

EFFECT OF OPPONENT'S PREEMPT

Do not let anyone tell you that they have a system of artificial gadgets that lands them in the right spot every time, despite preempts. It is not so. When you are ready to open the bidding with 1 ♦ on a neat fourteen- or fifteen-point hand and the player on your right blurts out 3 ♡, you simply have to admit that he has put you at a disadvantage. He has.

You may feel irritated and frustrated, but you must not let your opponent talk you into making a rash and desperate entry into the bidding just because you had a good opening bid.

There is a saying that the poker player who is never bluffed is a losing player. So is the bridge player who practically never passes an opponent's preemptive bid. "They're not going to keep *me* out of the bidding" sounds very good if you happen to land on your feet. But chances are you will not do so. And if a catastrophe occurs, partner will be justified in asking you if you have lost your mind.

If you can control the urge to be stampeded into taking unwarranted action after an opponent's preempt, you may be surprised (and consoled) to contemplate the fact that a great many such bids turn out badly—for the opponents. Your right-hand opponent may open the bidding with 3 ♡ on some such garbage as:

♠ 2   ♡ K J 9 7 4 3   ♦ 10 9 4 3   ♣ 9 8

This is a bid geared for trouble. You have a fair hand with a five-card spade suit to the ace-queen. You pass. Everybody passes. You lead something, and dummy comes down with K J 10 8 7 in spades and enough high cards to keep your partnership from making anything. However, dummy also has the lone deuce of hearts or possibly no hearts, and the 3 ♡ contract is down a couple of tricks.

I have seen this sort of thing happen many, many times, and it is odd that the partner of the preemptor almost always makes the same remark as he puts the dummy hand on the table: "Nice going, partner," he says in a voice bubbling with sarcasm. "You kept them out of the other major."

MORE EXAMPLES OF 4 NT BIDS

Getting back to our question "When is Blackwood Blackwood," consider this sequence:

WEST	NORTH	EAST	SOUTH
3 ♡	Double	4 ♡	4 NT

On the basis of usefulness, South's 4 NT bid must be the unusual notrump asking North to bid his better minor suit. North's double after the 3 ♡ opening promised ability to play spades and at least one other suit. When South by-passed spades, he was obviously saying that he did not think his side could play to advantage in that suit. This would leave only diamonds and clubs, and North would be expected to bid one of those suits at the five level. In a typical situation South's distribution would be two spades, one heart and five cards in each minor suit.

It comes down to this: The best use of any bid is that which will gain you the most points the most often.

Some players have difficulty interpreting the meaning of a 4 NT bid in an auction like this:

WEST	EAST
1 ♠	2 NT
3 ◇	3 NT
4 ◇	4 NT

Actually there should be no problem here if a little logic is applied to the situation. In the first place, East limited his hand when he bid 2 NT: He has from thirteen to fifteen high-card points and a balanced distribution. West's 3 ◇ call suggested that he believed the hand might play better at a suit rather than at notrump. When East failed to make a choice bid of 3 ♠ over 3 ◇, it is a practical certainty that he does not have as many as three spades in his hand. Also, his 3 NT bid indicated no interest in reaching a slam, because as far as he knows the 3 NT call will be followed by three passes. When he bids 4 NT over West's 4 ◇ it is a sign-off—he wants to play the hand there. His most likely distribution is two spades, four hearts, three diamonds and four clubs. His message is that he has a hand eminently suited for play at notrump and not too well suited for a slam. If West has some kind of wild distribution such as 6-1-6-0, plus good controls, he may go on. But East is not asking for aces with his 4 NT bid and West is on his own.

Here is another situation where the meaning of a 4 NT bid might not be quite clear. It involves intervention in a smooth bidding sequence by a pesky opponent:

SOUTH	WEST	NORTH	EAST
1 ♠	Pass	2 NT	4 ◇ *or* 4 ♡
4 NT			

South's 4 NT bid must be Blackwood. Let's say that he had slam aspirations and was planning to say 4 ♣ at his second turn (the 4 ♣ would be Gerber because partner's last bid was in notrump). Unable to bid 4 ♣ because of East's preempt, South had to revert to Blackwood to find out how many aces North held.

What if South had really wanted to play 4 NT? He could simply pass East's bid and leave it up to North. This pass would be absolutely forcing, as both North and South know that they have a total of 26 high-card points at a minimum, and possibly more. So it would be clear that it was their hand and that they should either go on and bid game somewhere or double East and punish him for his temerity.

Suppose that South passed but North doubled East's 4 ◇ (or 4 ♡) call. South could then bid 4 NT if he wished to play the hand there, and his intention would—or should—be clear to his partner.

SUMMING UP THE PROBLEM

From the abundance of "doubtful cases" that have been cited, it might appear that deciding whether partner's bids of 4 NT or 4 ♣ are really ace-asking is an almost hopeless task. Not so. In nine out of ten cases your partner's intentions will be crystal-clear. I have merely tried to offer some helpful suggestions concerning those doubtful cases which, incidentally, come up only rarely.

Usually, preempting opponents create the problems as to whether a bid is or is not conventional. But by means of some good hard thinking, those problems can almost always be solved by asking yourself the question: "Is the bid of 4 NT (or 4 ♣) likely to be useful more frequently in its conventional sense or in its natural sense?" If, on rare occasions, you do take a wrong view as to the meaning of partner's bid, you will have company.

If we could just get the rules changed so that our opponents would have to keep their mouths shut when we open the bidding, life would be much simpler. Or if we could arrange it so that we could bid "4 NT Blackwood" or "4 NT not Blackwood," that would be helpful. But I seriously doubt that we could ever have these changes effected.

When your opponents do not enter the bidding it is recommended that you treat all of your partner's bids of 4 ♣ as Gerber, asking for aces, when your immediately preceding bid was any number of notrump. On rare occasions partner may simply be trying to get to a game in clubs. But in that event he can bid 5 ♣ over your ace-showing response and you can let him play it there. Remember, if partner is really serious about a slam and wants to ask you how many kings you have, his follow-up bid after saying 4 ♣ is 5 NT, not 5 ♣. In other words, you go back to Blackwood to ask for kings.

6

Point Count Vs. Playing Tricks

♠ ♡ ◇ ♣

It is obvious that you need adequate controls to successfully fulfill a slam contract. The opponents have the first lead, and if they can win the first two tricks you are down before you even get the lead. But controls are not all you need. You must also have an adequate number of playing tricks.

The possession of four aces and four kings in your partnership is a pleasant setup, but they will win only eight tricks. For a slam you have to find four other tricks somewhere. So to undertake a slam you must determine that you and your partner have sufficient controls *and* sufficient playing tricks. The determination of the number of playing tricks comes first.

NEED TO DETERMINE PLAYING TRICKS

The point-count method of ace equals four, king equals three, queen equals two and jack equals one is in almost universal use today. This is an attempt to measure playing tricks by a mathematical formula. Although this method may not be the most accurate valuation to apply to these high cards, it is the simplest, for it avoids the use of fractions and the addition of large numbers. It is accurate enough except in rare cases—and particularly in the lower ranges of bidding.

But not only high cards take tricks. The additional ruffing value of trumps enables you not only to get control of the hand (gain the lead) but also to take tricks. And tricks can be won by establishing the small cards in long side suits and by various other devices such as the throw-in play or the squeeze. These additional trick-taking sources are best described as *distributional values*. Attempts to measure by point-count values the playing tricks that stem from distributional values have not been universally successful. Different authorities assign different values to distributional combinations, and the general disagreement on this subject is indicative of the difficulty in finding the correct values.

None of the attempts to measure the trick-taking potential of distribution by a point-count method give adequate consideration to this question: Do the partnership hands fit together well or are they misfits? Experienced players, after they pass the first or second round of bidding, tend to forget about point-count valuation for distribution. They measure how well their two hands fit, depending on the bidding sequence.

At the risk of being called old-fashioned (but practical, nevertheless) let's translate point-count valuation back to what it is supposed to represent—namely, playing tricks.

Suppose you open the bidding with 1 ♠, holding:

♠ A K 6 5 4   ♡ ——   ◊ Q 4 3 2   ♣ A J 5 4

If your partner's hand fits only fairly well with yours, you would be correct in making a preliminary estimate that your hand is worth something better than five playing tricks. Assuming fairly normal distribution around the table, you could reasonably figure on losing one spade and winning four tricks in that suit. You can win with the ace of clubs. And the queen of diamonds and jack of clubs are added values that may or may not help in winning other tricks.

If your partner's hand is a complete misfit with yours, then your hand is probably worth less than five-plus playing tricks.

However, if your partner's hand fits perfectly, your hand may easily be worth something like seven playing tricks.

So, as the bidding proceeds you may well change your mind

about how many playing tricks your hand is worth. Revaluation is the key to accurate determination of your trick-taking potential. Revaluation based on what your partner bids—or fails to bid.

AN EXAMPLE OF DRASTIC REVALUATION

As before, your hand is:

♠ A K 6 5 4   ♡ ——   ♢ Q 4 3 2   ♣ A J 5 4

Suppose your right-hand opponent passes, you bid 1 ♠ and your partner raises to 3 ♠. (For our purposes here, partner's raise is forcing to game, not the limit raise as used by many players today.) You now know that at least as far as the spade suit is concerned, your partner's hand does fit well with yours. But you still do not know how many playing tricks your hand is worth. If partner's outside strength is in hearts, you have a misfit and your hand is not worth seven playing tricks. But it *is* worth about that if partner's outside strength is in the minor suits.

Partner's hand could be:

♠ Q 10 3 2   ♡ A K 6   ♢ 7 6   ♣ K Q 7 2

His 3 ♠ bid has indicated that he has about five playing tricks. However, your hand and his will take only eleven tricks.

Now, to make the point clear about the value of "fitting" hands, reverse partner's holdings in the red suits. You now belong in a grand slam. You go from eleven tricks to thirteen *without increasing the high-card count even one point.*

Together you and your partner have only 28 points in high cards, somewhat less than the textbook requirement for a *small* slam. But when your hands fit well, your distributional tricks will make up for any shortage in high-card points for slam bidding. Where the two hands fit poorly, you will take fewer tricks.

In estimating your playing tricks, here is another important point to consider, one that may help you to avoid overvaluing your hand. *Your hand improves to a greater extent when partner strongly raises your long, weak suit than it does when he raises your long, solid suit.*

Suppose you open the bidding with 1 ♠ on a spade suit such as Q 7 6 4 3 2. A jump to 3 ♠ by partner makes this a terrific suit. But if your spade holding is A K Q 9 8 5, partner's raise to 3 ♠ does not improve your hand to any great extent. If he had only trey-deuce of spades, you could run off six spade tricks over two-thirds of the time. In addition to the four spades promised by partner's raise, he has to have ruffing values to make his four trumps really worthwhile. These ruffing values would consist of voids, singletons and doubletons in the side suits. Possibly he can show those values later in the auction.

Suppose you open the bidding with 1 ♠ on this hand:

     ♠ Q 7 6 4 3 2   ♡ A K 6 4   ◇ A 7   ♣ 3

Your preliminary estimate is that the hand is worth about six playing tricks, possibly a little less. You have to start somewhere, and of course you will revalue after hearing what partner has to say.

If partner's bidding indicates that he has a complete misfit (as where he bids and rebids clubs and shows no interest in the major suits), you had better drop your estimate back to not more than five playing tricks. But suppose partner's response is an immediate raise to 3 ♠. The great improvement in your trump suit, plus the upswing in your distributional values represented by the singleton and doubleton, make your hand worth about seven tricks. From a hand where you were doubtful about your side's ability to win as many as nine tricks anywhere, you are now in the slam zone. Now, and only now, are you in a position to check on first- and second-round controls to test for a slam.

So, for the purposes of translating point count into playing tricks, let's summarize it like this:

(1)   A flat hand such as 4-3-3-3 or 4-4-3-2 improves about one-half a trick when a good fit is found with partner.

(2)   A hand with moderate distribution such as 5-3-3-2 improves about one trick when a good fit is found.

(3)   A hand with extreme distributional advantages improves two tricks and sometimes even more when a good fit is found.

(4)   If the hand with extremely good distribution contains a long, nearly solid suit, it improves only about one trick when a good fit is found.

(5)   A hand with extremely good distribution containing a long, weak suit decreases sharply in value when the bidding indicates a misfit.

And here is a summary on evaluations of opening bids—before you are in a position to know whether there is a fit or a misfit. First let us consider those types of hands that we seem to get so often—those that do not have any suit over five cards in length and do not contain two suits of five cards or more.

(1)   A hand with thirteen high-card points is worth slightly over four playing tricks.

(2)   A hand with fifteen high-card points is worth about five playing tricks.

(3)   A hand with seventeen or eighteen high-card points is worth about six playing tricks.

(4)   Each card over five in any suit is worth an additional playing trick.

(5)   Possession of two five-card suits adds something more than one playing trick.

(6)   A hand with a long, solid suit is worth more playing tricks for an opening bid than a hand with a long, weakish suit, but does not improve so radically when a good fit is found.

In the following hand, a player had to make quite a drastic revaluation of his holding based on his partner's bidding. The partnership then proceeded cautiously but surely to the only game contract they could make.

NORTH
♠ 10 6 3
♡ 8 2
◇ Q 7 6 5 3 2
♣ A J

WEST
♠ K J 8
♡ Q 10 7 4
◇ 9 8
♣ K 9 5 4

EAST
♠ A 9 7 5 4
♡ 9 5
◇ 4
♣ Q 8 7 3 2

SOUTH
♠ Q 2
♡ A K J 6 3
◇ A K J 10
♣ 10 6

The bidding:

SOUTH	WEST	NORTH	EAST
1 ♡	Pass	1 NT	Pass
2 ◇	Pass	3 ◇	Pass
3 ♡	Pass	4 ♣	Pass
5 ◇	Pass	Pass	Pass

North did not think much of his hand when his partner opened the bidding with 1 ♡. He could take a trick with the ace of clubs and possibly with the jack, if his partner had the king or queen of that suit. He was deficient in his partner's heart suit, and his queen of diamonds was a doubtful value. All in all, North felt that he would be delighted with any plus score on the hand, however small.

But when South bid two diamonds at his second turn, the North hand shot up sharply in value (playing tricks). North could now assure his partner of full control of a trump suit—his queen of diamonds was a full winner, and he had plenty of trumps to ruff the third round of either hearts or clubs. Even so, he contented himself with a single raise of diamonds because South, up to this point, had promised nothing more than a minimum opening bid.

Actually, South was well above a minimum and his second bid of 2 ◇ had been a slight underbid. He now bid 3 ♡ on the theory that if his partner had three small hearts or something like queen doubleton it would be easier to make the heart game than the diamond game.

North still strongly preferred diamonds, but instead of going back to that suit directly he made the good call of 4 ♣. As his previous diamond raise had set that suit as the trump suit, it was easy to identify the club call as a cue-bid showing the club control. South then gave up on hearts and put the hand in a diamond game. Well bid!

It is too bad the play was not equally good. Let's take a look at it. (Although this is a book on slams, it will not hurt to digress a little. The declarer made a common error to lose his contract, and your study of it could earn you a lot of match points. Or money.)

West led the nine of diamonds and South won with the ace. He had nine tricks off top—six diamonds, the ace of clubs, the ace and king of hearts. The best and in fact the only reasonable line of play appeared to be to establish the heart suit. If that were possible, South could discard the jack of clubs from dummy on a good heart, then ruff his losing club.

Embarking on this plan, South drew the last outstanding trump, cashed the ace and king of hearts and ruffed a heart in dummy. East showed out on the third heart, proving that the defenders' hearts were split 4-2. But it was still all right as declarer needed to establish only one long heart to accomplish the club discard from the board.

South now came to his hand with a low diamond to the ten and ruffed another heart, making his fifth heart good. Only now did he realize the danger he was in. He was one entry short to his hand. He could lead a diamond to the jack (his last trump), play his good heart and sluff dummy's jack of clubs. But then the defenders could win three spade tricks.

The best he could do was to lead a spade from dummy, hoping the defenders would cash two spade winners before they knocked out the ace of clubs. As is the way of defenders, however, they did not do that. West killed the queen of spades with the king, shifted to a club and South was down one.

South's error in the play had to do with the matter of entries. He should not have cashed a second high diamond at trick two. He should have gone after the hearts immediately. Then he would be able to discard dummy's club loser on his fifth heart, earning his eleventh trick by ruffing dummy's third spade with his own last trump.

TAKING MAXIMUM ACTION

On rare occasions your own hand is so good and your partner's bidding is so strong that failure to have a fit in partner's principal suit should not deter you from taking what you might call maximum action. For example:

WEST	WEST	EAST
♠ A K J 10 8 2	1 ♠	3 ◇
♡ A Q	3 ♠	6 NT
◇ 3 2	?	
♣ Q J 8		

West has only trey-deuce in partner's diamonds, but partner leaped to 6 NT and could count on you for only thirteen points (West rebid spades, but that showed only a rebiddable spade suit, not necessarily anything over a minimum in high cards). Therefore East should have at least twenty high-card points. And instead of only thirteen points you have seventeen, plus an almost solid six-card spade suit.

East should have the queen of spades, which would ensure six tricks in that suit. If he does not have that card, his diamonds should be solid. Anyway, you have at least 37 high-card points in the partnership, leaving only three points for your opponents—and they may have less. West's lack of diamond help should be no problem in a situation like this, and West should unfailingly go on to 7 NT.

COUNTING CONTROLS

It is not sufficient to count winners. You must also try to determine how many losers you have. For instance, Q J 10 9 has two winners and obviously also has two losers. In other words, of the honor cards the aces and kings are the slam cards (guards). We call these cards *controls*.

A very common and very effective way of counting controls is as follows:

(1)   An ace is equal to two controls.

(2)   A king is equal to one control.

(3)   For playing in a suit contract

(a)   A void is equal to two controls, provided it can be established that it does not represent a duplication of values in partner's hand.

(b)   A singleton is equivalent to one control, provided it can be established that it does not represent a duplication of controls in partner's hand.

Controls are important on all hands. They are particularly important on those hands where there is "work to be done," suits to be established or crossruffs to be worked out. It frequently boils down to this:

(1)   To take ten tricks, it is well to have eight controls.

(2)   To take eleven tricks, it is well to have nine controls.

(3)   To take twelve tricks, it is well to have ten controls.

(4)   To contract for thirteen tricks, it is usually well to have at least eleven controls.

Bids of game or small slams should be made even when the odds only slightly favor making the contract. But grand slams should only be bid when the odds are overwhelmingly in their favor. Grand slams may become doubtful propositions unless you and your partner hold twelve controls.

(5)   With long, solid suits that need no establishing, you may be able to get by with fewer than the above-listed number of controls. A long, solid side suit in your hand may enable you to

create controls in the dummy by discarding losers on your solid suit.

These are not infallible rules. They are merely guides. You will notice that in each instance, you and your partner together need the number of controls equal to two less than the number of tricks you contract for. Obviously both of you should not be short more than one control.

In the early rounds of bidding when the sequence sounds slammish, it is well to stop and count your controls before proceeding full steam ahead. If your hand provides as many controls as it does playing tricks, you can usually go full steam ahead. If you have within one of as many controls as you have playing tricks, it is time to proceed with caution. If your controls fail by as many as two to equal the number of playing tricks you have, the red light is definitely on as far as slam-bidding is concerned.

These two hands are obvious examples:

(HAND I) ♠ A K Q 7 6   (HAND II) ♠ A K Q 7 6
          ♡ K Q 5 4   ♡ Q J 10 9
          ◇ A 8 3   ◇ 5 4
          ♣ 4   ♣ 8 3

Assuming reasonable trump support in the dummy, these hands might be said to be equal in their trick-taking value. Each hand seems to have seven playing tricks. But in other respects they are vastly different.

There are obviously more losing tricks in Hand 2 than in Hand 1. But the main difference is in the matter of controls. Hand 1 has six controls, plus another possible control in the singleton club. Hand 2 has only three controls. If your partner should respond 3 ♠ to your opening bid of 1 ♠, you would become very slam-minded with Hand 1, but no such thought would enter your head if you held Hand 2.

Thus the elements of successful slams are threefold:
    (1)   A sufficient number of winning tricks.
    (2)   Not too many losing tricks.
    (3)   A sufficient number of controls.

Controls mean that you and your partner must have enough aces, kings, singletons, void suits and other desirable assets that make it impossible for your opponents to win the first two tricks. If they cannot win the first two tricks, you have a chance. You may still have some work to do, but you have the possibilities of a squeeze, an end-play, an opponent's error and other assorted pieces of good fortune. If the opponents do take the first two tricks there is only one thing to do—improve your bidding.

SECONDARY ADVANTAGES OF HIGH CARDS

When you bid to a small slam it may be assumed that you and your partner hold most of the high cards in the deck. It is interesting to cogitate upon the fact that the *mere possession* of this plethora of aces, kings and queens gives you an advantage over your opponents above and beyond the mechanical point count. It furnishes you with the vital entries that enable you to slide back and forth easily and smoothly between your own hand and the dummy. Occasionally it enables you to finesse either way against a queen. And after the play of nine or ten tricks, you are frequently able to form a quite accurate idea as to which opponent holds that queen.

Since your abundance of high cards lets you retain the lead trick after trick, the opponents are forced to find safe discards. And it is a rather well-established fact that defenders do not always discard with absolute perfection. Retaining the lead, instead of having to surrender it every third or fourth trick as you would do in a lower contract, also gives you an advantage in getting an accurate count on the distribution of the opponents' hands. Since the opponents have very little in the way of high cards when you bid a small slam, they tend to protect those cards, sometimes to the detriment of their cause. For example, more than one slam has been made when a defender discarded a deuce from a holding of something like 10 8 3 2 and held onto a guard for a king in another suit. The declarer then ran four straight tricks in the first suit and turned up with a lone ace in the other.

Admittedly the advantages just outlined are somewhat intangible in nature. Nevertheless they are valid reasons why you should not wait until you are sure of twelve ice-cold tricks before embarking on a slam contract. The fruits of a slam, if you will pardon the expression, are such that some reasonable risk-taking is quite definitely justified. To repeat, you should be there if you have roughly a 50 percent chance for success.

7

Bidding to Slam

♠ ♡ ◇ ♣

THE DIRECT METHOD OF SLAM-BIDDING

Some wag defined this method as meaning "The direct route to the poorhouse." However, you do occasionally run across a hand where, for one reason or another, you decide to forgo the use of Blackwood, Gerber or any other artificial convention and simply leap into slam.

What you hope for, of course, is that the opening leader will get his hand on the wrong card, or that either defender will commit some other life-giving misdeed that will give you a chance for twelve tricks. When you successfully bring off a swindle like this it is unusually satisfying and even amusing— amusing to your partner, anyway. (Defenders have never been known to participate in the jollity.)

There is nothing wrong with an occasional gamble for a slam, especially if some kind of bluff bid is inserted in the early rounds of bidding that figures to tout your left-hand opponent off his best opening lead. The hardy souls who use this method consistently in rubber bridge games are brave. I find, however, that they also tend to be poor.

Here is an example of the direct method of reaching a slam:

NORTH
♠ K 9 8 2
♡ A Q J 8 7 6
◇ A
♣ Q 9

WEST   EAST
♠ 6   ♠ 5 4
♡ K 10 5 4   ♡ 9 3 2
◇ 10 9 7   ◇ Q 6 5 4 3
♣ K J 8 5 4   ♣ A 7 6

SOUTH
♠ A Q J 10 7 3
♡ ——
◇ K J 8 2
♣ 10 3 2

Here is how the bidding could have gone "scientifically":

SOUTH	WEST	NORTH	EAST
1 ♠	Pass	2 ♡	Pass
2 ♠	Pass	3 ◇	Pass
4 ◇	Pass	5 ♠	All pass

This hand is related to one shown previously, where a player with slam aspirations made sure his side had bid three suits and then jumped to five of a major. The message was that his partner should bid 6 ♠ if he did not have two quick losers in the unbid suit. In this current hand the South player did have two fast losers in the unbid suit, clubs, and therefore properly refused to go to the slam. As you see, five was the limit of the hand as the defenders can win two club tricks at the start—and the bidding tells them they can.

    The bidding on this same hand by a direct slam-bidder went as follows:

SOUTH	WEST	NORTH	EAST
1 ♠	Pass	2 ♡	Pass
2 ♠	Pass	6 ♠	All pass

West, fearing that a lead away from either of his kings would lose a trick, resorted to the "safe" opening of the ten of diamonds. After that there was not much to the play. The declarer was able to pitch one of dummy's clubs on his king of diamonds, establish dummy's hearts by ruffing in the closed hand and claim his twelve tricks.

On the surface it might appear that the best time to use the direct method of slam-bidding would be when you are playing against weak and inexperienced opponents. Not so. In the following deal, played in a national tournament in Cleveland several years ago, my partner, Stanley McComas, made a beautiful psychological bid based almost entirely on the knowledge that our opponents were very fine, thoughtful players.

This was the hand:

```
                    NORTH
                    ♠ K Q 8 6
                    ♡ 2
                    ◇ A K 10 9 4 3 2
                    ♣ A

  WEST                              EAST
  ♠ 7 2                             ♠ 9 3
  ♡ A 10 6 5 4                      ♡ Q 9 7 3
  ◇ 5                               ◇ Q 8 7
  ♣ K Q 10 5 4                      ♣ J 7 6 2
                    SOUTH
                    ♠ A J 10 5 4
                    ♡ K J 8
                    ◇ J 6
                    ♣ 9 8 3
```

My partner held the North hand, and the bidding proceeded
as follows:

NORTH (dealer)	EAST	SOUTH	WEST
1 ◇	Pass	1 ♠	Pass
3 ♣	Pass	3 ♠	Pass
4 NT	Pass	5 ◇	Pass
7 ♠!	Pass	Pass	Pass

West, on lead against the grand slam, thought a long time
but could not bring himself to lay down the ace of hearts. He
realized that North knew there was an ace off the hand—North
had found that out by bidding the Blackwood convention. Yet
North had unhesitatingly bid seven. North "had to be" void in
hearts! The fact that North had bid two suits and had leaped all
the way to seven in a third suit lent strength to this wrong view.
West could picture himself laying down the ace of hearts, getting
it ruffed in dummy and establishing the king in the South hand.
He could hear his partner saying: "How could you possibly
decide to lead the ace of hearts when the bidding clearly indicated the North hand was void in the suit?"

Anyway, West chose the king of clubs for his opening lead,
and thirteen tricks were easily available with the establishment of
dummy's diamonds.

My partner said later that he decided on his 7 ♠ bid for two
reasons. First, he thought we were having a good game, but not
good enough to land in the top money. Second, our opponents
were top-flight players. I think he was right. If the proverbial
little old lady had held the West hand she would have had that
ace of hearts out on the table before the echoes of the last pass
had died away in the distance, and she probably would have
doubled, too.

PRACTICING ECONOMY IN THE BIDDING

With all of our knowledge of Blackwood, Gerber and
cue-bids, plus many other recently created and more complicated

bidding gadgets, here is a word of warning guaranteed to improve your financial status, as well as your partner's temper: Do not use a lot of superscientific, "delicate-inference" bids unless it is absolutely necessary in order to acquire (or give) vital information. Keep your bidding as simple as you can. Make as few bids as possible. When you know where you are going, go there. Directly. Remember, your opponents are listening to every bid you make. Why give them a lot of free information that will clearly lay out their best defense?

To take a simple illustration, suppose you held a hand consisting of

♠ 2   ♡ A K J 9 8 6 5   ◇ 3 2   ♣ 10 9 2

If partner opens the bidding with 1 ♣, I suggest that you promptly bid 4 ♡. If your partner is any good at all, this bid will be as clear as crystal. It says that you have no interest in spades, no interest in notrump and little or no interest in clubs. You think you can make 4 ♡ if he has a decent opening bid. It could not be clearer if you showed partner your hand.

There is, of course, no reason why you should miss a slam. You did not say you thought you could make 5 ♡—or 6 ♡. Your bid said you thought you could make four opposite a minimum opening bid from partner. If he is well over a minimum and has the necessary controls, he can make the slam try. After all, he has "looked" in your hand and knows what to expect from you. If he does not—get a new partner. The danger in this situation and a thousand other related cases is not so much that you may miss a slam, but that your opponents will find a fine sacrifice bid at spades. This is what they may well do if your first bid is 1 ♡. Obviously it is much more difficult to find such a save when they have to make their first bid at the four level.

Consider this same principle in the context of a slam sequence:

NORTH
♠ J
♡ A 10 8 6
♢ A J 10 2
♣ Q J 8 4

WEST   EAST
♠ A Q 7 6   ♠ 10 9 8 5 4 3 2
♡ ——   ♡ 7 5 3 2
♢ 9 5 4   ♢ 8
♣ 10 9 7 6 5 2   ♣ 3

SOUTH
♠ K
♡ K Q J 9 4
♢ K Q 7 6 3
♣ A K

The bidding:

SOUTH	WEST	NORTH	EAST
1 ♡	Pass	3 ♡	Pass
?			

It would be a criminal miscarriage of slam-bidding tactics for South to say anything except 4 NT at his second turn. All he is interested in is the number of aces held by partner. Any attempt at "fancy stuff" could end in disaster. You can see the danger: If East and West ever get any clue concerning their spade fit, your slam goes down the drain.

If East got to play 6 ♠, the probable result would be down one—a beautiful save over the ice-cold heart slam. Perfect defense (opening a trump) would probably beat 6 ♠ two tricks—still a fine save. And if South cashed a club against 6 ♠ and then shifted to a trump, East could even make his contract, establishing West's clubs for the discard of a diamond and a heart from the East hand.

WATCH OUT FOR MISFITS

One mark of a good slam bidder is the ability to recognize, early in the bidding, that the hand may be a misfit and therefore dangerous for slam play, in spite of a wealth of high cards in the partnership.

The following is not the simplest example that could be offered, and many pairs in a tournament would reach the contract of 6 ♡ and go down one. But it does illustrate the subtle inferences that should be "caught" by a good partner.

```
                        NORTH
                        ♠ A K J 10 9
                        ♡ A
                        ◇ A 9 7
                        ♣ Q 8 7 6
        WEST                              EAST
        ♠ Q 8 7 4 3                       ♠ 6 5 2
        ♡ J 6                             ♡ 10 5 4 3
        ◇ 4 3                             ◇ J 8 6 5
        ♣ A 10 9 5                        ♣ J 3
                        SOUTH
                        ♠ ——
                        ♡ K Q 9 8 7 2
                        ◇ K Q 10 2
                        ♣ K 4 2
```

The bidding:

SOUTH	WEST	NORTH	EAST
1 ♡	Pass	2 ♠	Pass
3 ♡	Pass	3 NT	Pass
4 ◇	Pass	4 ♡	Pass
4 NT	Pass	5 ♠	Pass
6 ♡	Pass	Pass	Pass

The defense of the heart slam was quite simple. West cashed his ace of clubs and later there was no way to prevent East from winning a trump trick with his ten. Of course, six hearts could be a laydown. For one thing, the defenders' hearts could split 3-3. But that is against the odds. Also, North could have perfectly fitting cards like ace and queen of clubs and the two red aces. But the odds were against that, too, in view of North's bid in spades, and a jump bid at that.

North had a bit of a problem for his first bid. He thought of bidding only 1 ♠ considering the slight flaw of having only one of his partner's hearts. Looking ahead, however, he wondered what he would do at his next turn if South made the rather likely rebid of 2 ♡. A bid of 3 ♠ was no good as he did not quite have the hand or the suit for that call, and in fact South might conceivably pass it with an absolute minimum opener.

A 3 NT bid was out, too, as that bid could be made on only thirteen high-card points, and North had a total of eighteen points plus a good suit. All in all, North believed that a jump to 2 ♠ was the most practical call. It described the strength of his hand and made certain that the bidding would not be dropped under game.

Over 2 ♠ South might have bid 3 ♠ or 3 ♣. In either of these cases North would have taken some kind of bullish action. After his partner's actual rebid of 3 ♡, however, he immediately sensed danger. He tried to put on the brakes with a bid of 3 NT. This would have to be construed as a discouragement of slam attempts for the simple reason that, as far as North knew, the 3 NT call would be followed by three quick passes.

But South tried again. Over his 4 ◇ bid North had another hard decision. Clearly his partner had six hearts and only four diamonds. After considerable thought, North again made the weakest and cheapest bid possible, a return to 4 ♡.

At this point South should have placed considerable importance on the fact that his partner had not raised hearts at his first opportunity and had also declined to raise hearts even after they had been rebid. There was also the matter of South's void suit. Since his void was in a suit his partner had bid strongly, this was far from an asset—it was a serious liability.

Unimpressed by these considerations, South tried yet again.

He checked on aces, found that his partner had three, and put the hand in 6 ♡, where he went down one. And it served him right. Good defense would have beaten 6 ◊, and while 5 ◊ would probably be made, so would 5 ♡.

UNSCIENTIFIC SLAM BIDDING

On rare occasions you will encounter a hand where bluff or courage or whatever you want to call it could well serve you better than scientific bidding.

Consider this layout:

```
                        NORTH
                        ♠ Q 5 4
                        ♡ K Q J 9 8
                        ◊ 8
                        ♣ K 10 9 4
        WEST (dealer)                       EAST
        ♠ A K J 9 6                         ♠ 10 8 7 3 2
        ♡ 5 3                               ♡ 7
        ◊ J 2                               ◊ 7 6 5
        ♣ A Q 8 3                           ♣ 7 6 5 2
                        SOUTH
                        ♠ ——
                        ♡ A 10 6 4 2
                        ◊ A K Q 10 9 4 3
                        ♣ J
```

The bidding:

WEST	NORTH	EAST	SOUTH
1 ♠	2 ♡	Pass	?

South's decision as to what to bid will depend to a large extent on his evaluation of East as a player. East will be the opening leader against the obvious heart contract. If he is a stodgy, unimaginative, "bookish" player, I would bid 7 ♡ directly.

I really should not have to say it, but I suppose I had better: East *could* lead a club and South would be down one before he got started. On the other hand, East would be more likely to lead a spade ("I thought I ought to open *your* suit, partner"). Or he might lead a diamond. Or North might have the ace of clubs instead of just the king.

If you choose to get scientific in this type of situation, you might help East with his opening lead. For example, you might cue-bid the opponents's spades at your first opportunity, hoping your partner would consider this as inferentially promising good heart support and hoping also that partner would then bid clubs to show the ace of that suit. However, these tactics would probably eliminate the possibility of getting the favorable spade opening, and would narrow East's choices to diamonds and clubs. (Although we have labeled East as "unimaginative," he could hardly be bad enough to make the hopeless lead of a trump against this kind of bidding.) As you see, the grand slam is easy against anything except a club opening. East could not have the ace or the king-queen of clubs, for West and North would then not have the points for their bids.

Playing against an imaginative and expert East, the immediate jump to the grand slam would still have a good chance. He would probably not lead a spade, figuring you for a void when you bid seven hearts after hearing West bid 1 ♠. But it would be a 50-50 choice between diamonds and clubs. And, as stated, there is no reason why North could not have the ace of clubs plus a decent heart suit.

Against the good East player I would rather have a losing spade and a void in clubs! In other words, the old double swindle. If this touted East off the "hopeless" spade opening, the grand slam would be a laydown.

Please, no letters saying that you followed these recommendations and went down one when the opening leader got his hand on exactly the right card! I am guaranteeing nothing. I am merely suggesting that on freak hands where you have excellent and unusual support for a suit your partner has bid, go directly to the contract you think you have a good chance of making. Forget the super-scientific stuff in these cases. It could well guide the opening leader into making the only killing lead.

UNUSUAL SLAM TRIES

Blackwood or Gerber or cue-bids will serve you satisfactorily almost every time in your search for aces and kings in partner's hand. However, when you pick up an extremely freakish hand it may be impossible to find out about a specific ace or king by normal methods. In these cases the thing to do is to use a freakish bid.

For example, suppose you were the dealer and held this hand:

♠ K Q J 9 8 5 4 3 2   ♡ ——   ◇ ——   ♣ A K Q J

Your first reaction probably is that you never held a hand like this and do not think you ever will. However, there are many other hands, not quite so sensational-looking, where the same bidding principle would apply.

The suggested bid on the hand is 6 ♠. Partner should be able to figure out that you are interested *only* in high spade honors. If he has the ace of spades and nothing else, he should bid 7 ♠. Your opening bid said that you could win twelve tricks with spades as trump. If you were interested in aces and kings in the other suits you could have started out with a forcing bid of 2 ♠ (or 2 ♣ if you use weak two bids) and later used Blackwood. Since you did not do that, it should be absolutely clear that the lack of the ace of spades is the only reason you did not bid seven yourself.

If partner held:

♠ A   ♡ 5 4 3 2   ◇ 7 6 5 4   ♣ 6 5 3 2

he should bid 7 ♠ without blinking an eye.

If he held:

♠ 6   ♡ A K Q 5   ◇ A Q J 9   ♣ 10 9 8 7

he should pass.

Moving the bidding level down one notch, your best bet with the following hand is to open with 5 ♣ :

♠ Q J 10 9 8 6 4 2   ♡ A K Q 10   ◇ A   ♣ ——

Again, just a minimum amount of thinking should convince your partner that you are interested only in high honors in the bid suit. If you were interested in other aces and kings you could easily find out about them by using the Blackwood Convention. Four spades would make game—there is no bonus for making five. Therefore your hand must be cold for five, and the ace or king of spades in partner's hand would make it six.

You will note that the last hand is not quite as impossible-looking as the preceding one. For one thing, your four-card side suit is A K Q 10 instead of A K Q J. But a player with any red blood at all would and should open the last hand with 5 ♠. His partner could have the jack of hearts, or an opponent could have it as a singleton or doubleton or as part of a three-card holding. Or you might get a heart opening lead. Or you might even be able to ruff the ten of hearts in dummy. But if it bothers you, take out the ten of hearts and put the jack back in—we are only talking about general principles anyway.

In addition to telling partner *specifically* what you want him to have to raise you, there is another advantage in opening the bidding with five or six of a major on hands like this. In view of the wild distribution of your hand, it is odds-on that the opponents' hands are also extremely unbalanced. If your partner has no points your opponents could well have a good sacrifice at the six or seven level. In the last hand shown, for example, you have only 16 points in high cards. Somebody has to have the other 24. If it is the opponents, you want to keep them out of the bidding.

And however brave you are, you must admit it is quite hard to
overcall an opening bid of something like 6 ♠.

In the last two examples, notice that we have made the long,
dominant suit a major. An opening bid of 6 ◇ or 6 ♣ would
have the same meaning as a bid of 6 ♠ or 6 ♡. However, down at
the five level an opening bid in a minor has an entirely different
meaning.

An opening call of 5 ◇, for example, is simply a preemptive
bid. It is an effort to make it difficult for the opponents to reach
their best spot. It is a conscious and purposeful overbid. It
promises ability to win eight or nine tricks, depending on vulnerability. (With some players it promises ability to win six or seven
tricks, but since this is a book aimed at improving your game and
not ruining it, we will move gingerly past that concept!)

A bid of 5 ♣ or 5 ◇ belongs to the same family as a bid of
3 ♡ or 4 ♣. The only difference is that it promises the ability to
take more tricks with the named suit as trump. Not vulnerable,
against vulnerable opponents, an opening bid of 5 ◇ would be a
resonable shot on:

♠ 2   ♡ ——   ◇ K Q J 10 8 6 4 3   ♣ J 10 9 7

If you get doubled, the most you can go for is three tricks
—500 points. And if the opponents can win five tricks against
this hand, chances are very good that they could make a game,
which would be worth more than 500 points. If they go on and
bid and make a slam, you have to console yourself with the
thought that you did the best you could to keep them out of it.

8

Slam Bidding after Opening 1 NT

♠ ♡ ◇ ♣

HISTORY OF THE NOTRUMP BID

Back in the early 1930s when Ely Culbertson was the reigning king of bridge, the opening bid of 1 NT was quite unfashionable. If you used it in preference to a suit-bid opening you were looked upon as something of a heretic. The "Approach-Forcing" system was the big thing. Mr. Culbertson wrote in one of his books:

"Even with a hand such as:

♠ A Q 3 2   ♡ A J 6   ◇ K 10 4   ♣ K J 4

an opening bid of 1 ♠ is far more scientific than an opening 1 NT bid, in spite of the fact that the hand is distributed 4-3-3-3 and that every suit is in tenace position."

As time passed, the notrump opening gained in favor and popularity. For many years, however, most authorities held to the dictum that the bid should be made only with hands distributed 4-3-3-3 or 4-4-3-2, and that all four suits must contain stoppers. Later, the requirements were relaxed—you could bid 1 NT with just three suits stopped, and with a five-card suit (the five-carder had to be a minor). Today, many good players open 1 NT with five cards in any suit, and with a worthless doubleton in one suit.

There are two reasons for the increasing popularity of the 1 NT opening. First, it is an exceptionally descriptive call, giving partner a wealth of useful information about your hand in one fell swoop. Partner immediately knows that you have no void suit, no singleton, no six-card or longer suit. He knows that you probably have reasonable support for any suit he chooses to bid, and he knows within very narrow limits the extent of your high-card strength. What other opening bid is this informative? In addition, the notrump opening is preemptive to a degree. For example, your opponents may have a good spot in the heart suit. If you open with 1 ◇, your left-hand opponent would bid 1 ♡. But if you open with 1 NT he may not have the courage (or the cards) to overcall in hearts at the two level.

The second reason for the increasing popularity of 1 NT openings is that this bid solves the opener's rebid problem. Take this hand, for example:

$$ \spadesuit A Q 6 \qquad \heartsuit K J 8 \qquad \diamondsuit K 96 \qquad \clubsuit K J 92 $$

If you open this hand with 1 ♣ you run into real trouble trying to find a good rebid if partner responds with a bid of one in any of the other three suits. Your hand is too strong for a rebid of 1 NT and not strong enough to jump to 2 NT. It is too strong for a single raise of partner's suit and not strong enough (or long enough in the trump department) for a double raise. You simply look ahead, anticipate this dilemma and open the bidding with 1 NT. With the information this call gives your partner about your distribution and your general strength, he can act with considerable accuracy and confidence.

I go along heartily with the current admiration for the notrump opening and the way the requirements for the bid have been liberalized, although I must confess to some slight feeling of uneasiness when a hand contains a five-card major suit and a worthless doubleton.

THE FIFTEEN TO SEVENTEEN POINT NOTRUMP

For some years the ideal limits for an opening bid of 1 NT have been considered sixteen to eighteen points. We have already

discussed the rebid problem faced by the player who opens a
fairly balanced sixteen-point hand with one of a suit and gets a
one-over-one response from his partner. Actually, the rebid
problem starts with fifteen points and ends with seventeen points.
If you do not already use fifteen to seventeen points for your
opening notrump range, you will profit by changing over.
Consider this hand:

♠ A J 8   ♡ K J 7   ◇ Q 9 7 6   ♣ A 10 7

Say you open the bidding with 1 ◇ and partner responds
with 1 ♡ or 1 ♠. Do you really think you would be doing full
justice to this hand by giving partner a single raise in the suit he
bids? And if you elect to rebid 1 NT with your hand, how can
partner know that you are as good as you are in high-card
strength? (With an eighteen-point hand you are strong enough to
say 2 NT over partner's one-over-one response.) As far as partner
knows, when you rebid 1 NT you have a minimum thirteen-
point opening or possibly twelve high-card points and some kind
of a five-card suit. It would be quite easy to miss a makeable
3 NT contract.
Change the hand shown above to:

♠ A J 6   ♡ K J 8   ◇ K Q 9 7   ♣ A 10 7

This time 1 ◇ *is* your best opening. With eighteen high-
card points you are slightly strong for a 1 NT bid. If partner bids
1 ♡ or 1 ♠, your rebid is 2 NT. With partner's promised six (or
more) points, you have at least 24 points in the partnership,
leaving the opponents a maximum of 16. It should be possible to
make 2 NT. Partner does not have to bid again, for by inference
your jump to 2 NT expressed the inability to jump to 3 NT. If he
has a reasonably balanced hand and just enough for his first bid,
he will pass.
When you open the bidding with 1 NT and partner jumps
to three in any suit, he is showing a good suit and a good hand.
His bid says he knows that a game can be made, and he could

well have a slam in mind. With only two cards in partner's suit, your best bet is to rebid 3 NT. With three or more cards in partner's suit, headed by ace, king or queen, it is usually best to raise partner.

One exception to this would be the case where your 1 NT opening was an absolute minimum, with your high-card count made up principally of queens and jacks. For example, if you opened the bidding with 1 NT on this hand:

♠ A Q 6   ♡ Q J 2   ◊ Q J 6   ♣ Q J 10 2

and partner bid 3 ♡, you might do well to take the conservative course and go back to 3 NT in spite of the fact that you have three hearts including the queen. In general, queens and jacks are notrump cards. Aces and kings are the slam cards.

For another example, assume that you opened the bidding with 1 NT and partner bid 3 ♡. Your hand:

♠ A K 9   ♡ K 10 3   ◊ A 9 8 6   ♣ Q 8 7

Your best action would be to raise hearts, but you should not do so directly. In this situation you can give partner two pieces of information for the price of one. Your bid with this hand is 3 ♠. This says: "Partner, I am willing and able to raise you to 4 ♡, but along the way I may as well mention that my principal high-card strength is in the spade suit." Exchange the spade and club holdings in your hand, and your most informative and helpful bid over partner's 3 ♡ would be 4 ♣.

Your rebid of 3 ♠ on the hand shown above would be especially helpful to partner if his hand was

♠ 3 2   ♡ A Q 7 6 4 2   ◊ 2   ♣ K J 10 2

He would learn that you held at least three hearts headed by the king, and that there was no danger of losing the first two tricks in the spade suit. There would be an excellent chance of reaching a makeable 6 ♡ contract with only 26 high-card points in the partnership. You might possibly miss the slam, but you certainly have much less chance of getting there if you simply raise partner directly to 4 ♡. His worthless doubleton in spades would probably deter him from taking any further aggressive action.

To sum up, when you open the bidding with 1 NT and partner jumps to three of a suit, there are only two "classes" of bids for you to consider. These are:

(1) 3 NT or (2) any other bid.

The 3 NT rebid says: "Partner, I do not have three cards to a high honor in your suit." Any bid other than 3 NT says: "Partner, I have at least three cards in your suit headed by a high honor and am willing to raise you to four. If I bid some other suit instead of raising you directly, I am saying that I have the ace of the suit I bid and probably other high cards as well."

9

Notrump Slams

♠   ♡   ◇   ♣

There appears to be an enormous amount of ignorance concerning the bidding of notrump slams. The prevailing thought, especially among players of modest experience, is that if you bid two suits and your partner bids the other two suits and neither partner can raise the other, then the "obvious" solution is to get into notrump. If there is a wealth of high-card strength in the partnership, this sort of thinking often results in a contract of 6 NT. What else?

Here is a horrible example that I observed at a recent tournament:

NORTH
♠ A K J 5 4
♡ 5 4 3
◇ A Q 3 2
♣ 2

WEST
♠ 9 7 3
♡ J 10 8 2
◇ K 8
♣ 10 9 6 5

EAST
♠ Q 10 8 2
♡ 7 6
◇ J 10 9 7
♣ Q 7 3

SOUTH
♠ 6
♡ A K Q 9
◇ 6 5 4
♣ A K J 8 4

North was the dealer and the bidding went like this:

NORTH	EAST	SOUTH	WEST
1 ♠	Pass	2 ♣	Pass
2 ♦	Pass	4 NT!	Pass
5 ♡	Pass	6 NT	All pass

There are some players (very few, thank heaven) who read bridge books and columns not for education and not for the fun of it, but mainly for the purpose of searching eagerly for flaws so they can write an irate letter to the author. For the benefit of these technical geniuses, let us admit at the start that you can make 6 NT on this hand if every finesse works and every suit breaks favorably.

No one will argue with the statement that North had a sound opening bid. In fact, he was a little over a minimum. He might have had thirteen points and a four-card suit, but instead he had fourteen points and a good five-card suit.

South bid 2 ♣ and heard his partner say 2 ♦. With a powerful holding in hearts, the suit nobody had yet bid, South bulled the hand into a small slam at notrump.

West led the jack of hearts and South won with the queen. Getting his first good break, South for unknown reasons decided to go after clubs rather than spades. He led his lone spade to dummy's ace, returned a club and finessed the jack. When this held he cashed the ace and king of clubs and gave up a club in order to establish his fifth card in the suit.

West won the fourth club and returned a spade. South went up with dummy's king, led a heart to his king and cashed his fifth club and the ace of hearts. He then led a diamond and finessed dummy's queen. That worked, too. But after he cashed the ace of diamonds, East won the last trick with the queen of spades over dummy's jack.

South was extremely fortunate to go down only one. He was lucky in deciding to go after clubs first rather than spades. If he had first finessed the jack of spades he never would have made his fifth club because that involved giving up the fourth round of clubs. The queen of clubs was right and the clubs broke evenly. To top it off, the diamond finesse worked. But even with these unusual strokes of good fortune, the result was down one.

If everything was wrong on this hand—every finesse failing and every suit breaking badly—it is almost too brutal to contemplate what the final result would have been. South would be lucky to win more than nine tricks.

POINT COUNT AND NOTRUMP SLAMS

Let us change the South hand a little. South will retain the same high cards but we will make some changes in their location.

NORTH (same hand)	SOUTH (new hand)
♠ A K J 5 4	♠ Q 9
♡ 5 4 3	♡ A K 8
◇ A Q 3 2	◇ K J 4
♣ 2	♣ A 10 9 8 6

The hand contains the same high cards as before—two aces, two kings, a queen and a jack. Coupled with the same North hand shown before, you now have *twelve* tricks off the top, barring a monstrously bad break in the spade suit.

Think about this. The textbooks say that a small slam can usually be made if a partnership has 33 points in high cards. It is not enough to say just that, for it presupposes a reasonable fit in at least two suits. If you have a hand that fits very well you can often make a small slam with somewhat less than 33 points. For example, in the hand just shown, North and South had only 31 high-card points. And if the partnership hands fit badly, you may well go set with even more than 33 points. So remember, high cards in a suit bid by your partner are like gold. In a suit your partner bids *and rebids,* the valuation goes up to platinum.

Small slams at notrump are dangerous and must be handled with great care. Of course at duplicate bridge you should give serious consideration to such contracts as you will get a higher score than you would get for bidding and making six of a suit. For a vulnerable small slam in a minor suit your score is 1370; for making six of a major you get 1430; and for making a small slam in notrump you earn 1440. Only ten points difference between a major suit and a notrump slam. Yet if nobody else reaches 6 NT you have an absolute top score.

This is a good place to repeat a bit of advice previously given. Point count for high cards (four for an ace, three for a king, etc.) is very useful and quite accurate in the lower ranges of bidding. But its accuracy slowly ebbs away as you get up into the slam zone.

You may hear a player remark in an off-hand fashion, "That hand will make 3 NT or 4 NT." Nobody sees anything unusual in this since, assuming you bid 3 NT, you get the same score whether you make three or four. But if someone made a similar remark about slams you would be justified in considering him some kind of a nut. If you bid 7 ♠ and make six you have earned yourself a zero score. If you bid six and make a laydown seven you are not much better off.

CONSIDERATIONS OTHER THAN ACES AND KINGS

In contemplating a small slam at notrump there are other important things to think about in addition to aces and kings. The main considerations are suit length, suit solidity and high cards in suits bid by partner.

To point up the importance of ten-spots and of five-card (or longer) suits in trying to make 6 NT contracts, consider these three partnership hands:

HAND I	♠ A Q 8 4	♠ K J 7
	♡ K J 8	♡ Q 7 3
	◇ A Q 7	◇ K 9 2
	♣ A K 6	♣ J 7 4 3
HAND II	♠ A Q 7	♠ 8 6 4 3
	♡ J 7 3	♡ A K Q
	◇ A J 6 4	◇ Q 3
	♣ A Q 7	♣ K J 4 2

HAND III ♠ K 5 4 2   ♠ Q J 6
        ♡ J 8 6 3   ♡ A Q 4
        ◇ Q J 9   ◇ A K 8
        ♣ K Q   ♣ A J 9 8

Observe that each set of partnership hands contains 33 high-card points. Notice also, however, that none of the hands contains a ten-spot or a five-card suit. In Hand 1 you can win eleven tricks—four spades, two hearts, three diamonds and the two top clubs. You will make the slam only if you are lucky enough to drop a doubleton queen in the club suit, and the odds are sharply against that good fortune. However, add the ten of clubs to either hand and you will have a legitimate finesse against the queen. This would be a 50-50 shot and a reasonable risk in view of the possible reward involved.

Hand 2 is a little harder to analyze. To be fair, let's say that the spade finesse wins and the diamond finesse loses. You will then win eleven tricks—two spades, three hearts, two diamonds and four clubs. Add the ten of diamonds to either hand and that suit would produce your twelfth trick.

If the king of hearts is behind the ace-queen in Hand 3, you will almost surely be set at 6 NT, no matter how you play. So let's say the king of hearts is right. You still do not have twelve tricks! You can win four clubs, three diamonds, two hearts and two spades. Again, add the ten of spades to either hand and, after knocking out the ace, you will have three winners in that suit instead of two.

It must be admitted that some 33-point hands will develop a sure twelve tricks even though they do not contain extra values in the form of good intermediate cards or long suits. And some 37-point hands with no extra values will make grand slams. But just remember, the odds are not in your favor.

Consider this layout:

        WEST   EAST
        ♠ A J 2   ♠ K 6 4
        ♡ A 6 5 4   ♡ K 7 2
        ◇ A 3 2   ◇ K J 6 5
        ♣ K Q J   ♣ A 5 4

Probably quite a few pairs in a tournament would reach a contract of 6 NT. All the aces and all the kings are accounted for, and the two hands have a total of 33 high-card points. Nevertheless it is a bad slam to be in. It will make if the spade finesse works, if the diamond finesse works (aw, come on!) and if the opposing hearts split 3-3. Just those three things. But if one of them fails, you take a minus score on a really beautiful hand. It would be quite a temptation, but most good bidders would stay out of this slam.

On the last hand some bidders reached 6 NT on the textbook high-card count of 33 points. In the following hand (admittedly slightly exaggerated to make the point clear), we depend on judgment. And of the two, I will take the latter every time.

WEST (dealer)	EAST
♠ A K J 10 9 8	♠ Q
♡ 3 2	♡ K 5 4
◇ A Q 10	◇ K 4 3 2
♣ 10 2	♣ A K Q J 3

The bidding:

WEST	NORTH	EAST	SOUTH
1 ♠	Pass	2 ♣	2 ♡
3 ♠	Pass	4 NT	Pass
5 ♡	Pass	6 NT	All pass

Let's figure that we are holding the East hand. Partner bids 1 ♠ and we say 2 ♣. Partner now bids 3 ♠, and in response to our 4 NT bid he shows two aces. We are now sure of twelve tricks—six spades, four clubs and the ace and king in one of the red suits. We do not care which red suit. To put it another way, we know we can take tricks not only with our aces and kings but with the nine and eight of spades and probably the trey of clubs as well. Maybe we do not know for sure that our partner's two lowest spades are the nine and eight, but when he bid spades and then *jump* rebid them, and did not have the queen, he figures to

have just what the diagram of the hand shows. Our trey of clubs
will probably be a winner because the lead of the four top honors
should pick up all of the clubs held by the defenders. Of course
we do not need that trick as we are already sure of twelve, but I
mention it to stress the point of the value of suit solidity. We also
know, by the use of the Blackwood Convention, that we cannot
hope to win all thirteen tricks. But South had better cash his ace
of hearts at trick one or he will not get it.

There is another good point in this hand. While a slam at a
suit is usually safer than a slam at notrump, in a case like the one
just illustrated, 6 NT is safer because of the danger of an adverse
ruff. South, who bid two hearts and cannot have too much in the
way of high cards, could well have a seven-card suit. If so, his
partner has a singleton heart and could ruff the second round of
that suit.

This is not to criticize the statements in the textbooks that
33 points in a partnership justify reaching a small slam. If you
have to say it briefly, that is about as close as you can get. For
one thing, it means that your opponents cannot have two aces.
The fact remains, however, that if you bid 33-point small slams
without any ten-spots or five-card suits in the partnership, well
over half of them will be set. If you care to test this, take 26 cards
from a deck and leave in enough high cards to total 33. Be sure
not to include the good intermediate cards (tens and nines). And
when you shuffle and deal these 26 cards into two hands, change
them around, if necessary, so that neither hand will have a
five-card or longer suit. If you have the patience and interest to
deal out a goodly number of such hands, you will find that six
will not be makeable most of the time.

Consider holding K Q J 3 2 in a single suit. The most
tricks you could hope to take at a notrump slam if partner has a
singleton would be two. Of course, if the opponents' cards were
split as evenly as possible you could take three (losing the first
and fourth rounds, then making your fifth card). But by that
time you would be down one. If the trey and deuce were changed
to the ten and nine you would count no "points" for those new
cards—but you would now win a sure four tricks in the suit. Or,
if partner held something like 10 5 4, you would win four
tricks in the suit most of the time. So count your good intermediate cards in reaching for a slam—mentally, if not arithmetically

10

The In-between Hand

♠ ♡ ◇ ♣

When your partner opens the bidding with one of a major suit and you have a good hand and good four-card or better support for that suit, there are three general types of action you can take in an effort to describe your holding.

Suppose partner opens the bidding with 1 ♠ and your hand is:

♠ K J 6 3   ♡ K 7 6   ◇ Q 2   ♣ A 9 8 2

You have about the equal of an opening bid and good spade support, and your correct call is 3 ♠. If partner merely bids 4 ♠, you will of course take no further action.

Again you get a 1 ♠ opening from partner and your hand is:

♠ K J 9 8   ♡ 6   ◇ A 10 3   ♣ A K Q J 2

This time you should bid 3 ♣, promising about nineteen points or more and indicating sharp interest in a slam.

This leads us to the type of hand that is somewhere in-between the two just described. West opens the bidding with 1 ♠ and this is the setup:

WEST   EAST
♠ A Q 5 3 2   ♠ K 7 6 4
♡ A 9 2   ♡ 5
◇ K 10 2   ◇ A 9 3
♣ 10 3   ♣ A Q 9 8 2

Here East has a hand that is too strong for a jump raise to
3 ♠ and not strong enough for a jump takeout in another suit.
This hand is best handled in the following manner:

WEST	EAST
1 ♠	2 ♣
2 ♠	3 ◊
3 NT	4 ♠

With a minimum opening bid, West's first rebid is 2 ♠. East
is still not ready to raise spades, so he bids 3 ◊. (Although East's
diamonds are not strictly biddable, there is no danger in this call.
East can always go back to spades without raising the level of
bidding if West happens to raise diamonds.) Again West gives
evidence of having opened a minimum hand by making his
weakest possible bid, 3 NT. Now, at long last, East shows his fine
spade support by bidding four in that suit.

It is only at this point that West knows his partner's previous bids were made for the purpose of showing high-card
strength and distribution, and knows that East was aiming for a
spade contract all the time. If West now bids 4 NT it should be
considered as Blackwood, asking for aces.

This is somewhat unusual in that West's rebids of 2 ♠ and
3 NT were of the minimum variety and showed absolutely no
interest in a slam. Looking at West's hand we see a spade suit
that could hardly be called robust, a minimum thirteen points in
high cards and no particular fit in what appears to be East's
principal suit, clubs. No wonder West put on the brakes after
opening the bidding.

However, when East finally raises spades, West gets an
entirely different picture of the partnership's 26 cards. West now
can count on good spade support and a good club suit. Thus
from a situation in which he was not even sure that a game
contract would be successful, West is now entitled to have slam
aspirations. He may not make a spade slam on the hand, but he
should have a very good chance for it (either by a successful
finesse in clubs or by establishing dummy's clubs by ruffing the
third round).

This is the type of slam that would probably be missed by half the field in a tournament. Note that there are only 26 high-card points in the partnership—far short of the 33 points mentioned in the textbooks. An almost perfect fit between the two hands is the answer, plus expert description of his strength and distribution by the responding hand.

Another situation that appears to be similar to the forgoing but actually is not is illustrated below:

WEST	EAST
♠ A K J 8 7	♠ 3 2
♡ 2	♡ Q J 10 6
◇ A K J 10 4	◇ Q 8 6
♣ Q 7	♣ K J 9 8

The bidding:

WEST	EAST
1 ♠	1 NT
3 ◇	3 NT
4 ◇	4 NT

East's first bid of 1 NT shows a weakish hand with no particular interest in game, let alone slam. Partner shows a fine hand with a jump rebid of 3 ◇, and again East makes the weakest possible response, 3 NT. When partner now bids 4 ◇, East's 4 NT call is not Blackwood but a suggestion that the hand will play best (and gain the highest score) by playing at 4 NT. The reason is that the 4 ◇ bid is no new information. East already knew his partner had diamonds.

Of course, West can go on if he has the hand for it and cannot stand notrump. If he does continue bidding he is obviously afraid of one of the two unbid suits, hearts and clubs. However, West should be able to count on East for at least potential double stoppers in those suits.

11

Action After A Game-level Jump Response

♠ ♡ ◇ ♣

There seems to be a widespread misinterpretation of the phrase "shutout bid." Take the sequence

WEST	EAST
1 ♠	4 ♠

West passes 4 ♠ and a slam is missed. You often hear West say something like, "Sorry partner, but I took your 4 ♠ call for a shutout bid and I thought you were telling me to keep quiet."

Every bridge writer at one time or another has probably stated that the words "never" and "always," and other "absolutes," do not belong in the lexicon of bridge. This may be true, but you could *almost* say that there is no such thing as a shutout bid! At least, not in the sense that the West player meant it in the above example.

East's 4 ♠ call was a shutout bid *only as far as he was concerned*. East was satisfied to play at 4 ♠ and not get any higher. But it would be arrogance of the worst sort if he expected his partner to pass with every conceivable hand.

As a matter of fact, East did not mean his bid that way. When he jumped to 4 ♠ he was merely describing his hand. The typical hand on which responder would raise opener's bid of one in a major to four would look like this:

♠ K 10 7 6 4   ♡ 2   ◇ A J 9 8 5   ♣ 9 7

He has good distribution that includes five trumps, a singleton and not more than nine high-card points.

If East intended to shut out *anybody,* it was the opponents —who would find it quite difficult to make their first bid at the five level.

Another sequence of bidding that often results in missing a slam is the case where opener bids one of a suit and responder says 3 NT. Many players consider the 3 NT call as a "sign-off" or "shutting off the bidding." This is not the case at all. The requirements for this jump to 3 NT are rather rigid. It is best used to show a hand distributed 4-3-3-3, with a high card (or cards) in every suit and a high-card count of from sixteen to eighteen points.

Opener is not justified in giving up on the possibility of a slam. He knows his partner cannot trump anything, but he also knows that partner can furnish reasonable support for any suit, including at least one high card. Therefore opener can try a second suit, if he has one, with the comfortable feeling that partner has at least three cards in that suit to an honor and that there is absolutely no chance of a misfit.

Here is a recent hand where a slam was reached in spite of the fact that the opening bidder had a minimum in high cards.

	WEST	EAST
♠	A Q 10 7 6	K 8 5
♡	4	K J 2
◇	J 8	A Q 2
♣	A Q 9 6 5	K 10 8 2

The bidding:

WEST	EAST
1 ♠	3 NT
4 ♣	4 ♡
6 ♣	Pass

East's 3 NT bid was also a minimum. He had sixteen high-card points (he might have had 17 or 18). Opener had only thirteen high-card points, but he had distributional advantages. Note that when he bid 4 ♣ this was *not* showing his second suit. Not yet. The 4 ♣ call was a Gerber bid asking for aces, because partner's last bid was in notrump. East bid 4 ♡, showing one ace, and West then bid 6 ♣. This last call *was* showing a second suit and the message was clear that West wanted his partner to choose at the six level between spades and clubs. East, with four clubs and three spades, had an easy choice. He passed.

The opening leader cashed the ace of hearts and shifted to a diamond. Declarer put up dummy's ace, picked up the trumps in three leads and parked his second diamond on the king of hearts.

As you see, there were only 29 high-card points in the partnership. But, West *knew* that the hands fit well as soon as he heard his partner say 3 NT. Far from being a sign-off, the 3 NT bid was highly encouraging to the opening bidder, who was fully justified in trying for a slam if he had more than a minimum either in high cards or in distributional advantages. As a matter of fact, the two hands could have fit even better than they did. East had four high-card points in the heart suit. If he had held the ace and two small hearts he still would have had four high-card points in that suit, but now the hand would have a good play for a grand slam.

Here is a hand in which the responder (East) tried for a slam and made it on a finesse, holding only nine high-card points, no aces and a weakish trump holding. He took this aggressive action because he did not make the mistake of interpreting his partner's strong second bid as a sign-off or shutout bid.

WEST	EAST
♠ A Q 9 3	♠ K 10 6 5 4
♡ 10 2	♡ K 4
◊ A K J 8	◊ Q 6
♣ A Q 8	♣ J 10 7 4

The bidding:

WEST	EAST
1 ◊	1 ♠
4 ♠	4 NT
5 ♠	6 ♣
Pass	

West's 4 ♠ call was not an auction-closing bid and he did not mean it that way. It simply meant that he thought 4 ♠ was makeable if East had as little as six high-card points and a biddable four-card spade suit. Another way to put it is that West thought he could win eight tricks at spades (high cards and ruffing ability) if East could just win two.

Instead of six points and a four-card spade suit, East had nine points and a five-card spade suit. In addition, he had a high card in his partner's first-bid suit, diamonds. And we have already stressed the point that high cards in partner's bid suits are worth their weight in gold.

The slam was no laydown, but if defenders failed to cash their ace of hearts at trick one, declarer could pick up the trumps (assuming no worse than a 3-1 spade break) and discard both of his hearts on dummy's diamonds. He would then have a play for a grand slam. If the opening leader got off to a club lead, the most sensible and practical play would be to refuse the finesse and go up with dummy's ace. East could then pick up the trumps, discard two hearts on dummy's diamonds, concede a trick to the king of clubs and claim the slam.

The play is interesting, but not too important for our purposes here. The main point is that when your partner makes a strong bid at the game level, he is by no means trying to discourage you from trying for a slam. If you have more than your previous bid or bids have promised, you should go on. The type of assets that should urge you on are controls in the unbid suits (aces, kings and singletons), high cards in suits your partner has bid—and courage.

Here is a hand where the responder (East) went on to a slam even though he had a miserable trump suit headed by the jack.

WEST	EAST
♠ A K Q 6	♠ J 5 4 3 2
♡ 5 4	♡ A 7 6
◇ A Q 7 2	◇ K 6 5
♣ K Q 2	♣ A 5

The bidding:

WEST	EAST
1 ♦	1 ♠
4 ♠	4 NT
5 ♡	6 ♠
Pass	

Offsetting the awful weakness of East's trump suit were the facts that he held first-round control in both of the suits that nobody had bid—plus the very important king of diamonds, a suit bid by his partner.

This slam was a laydown; East lost just one heart trick. Many players would miss this slam because of the weakness of their spade suit. The trick is to consider your side's 26 cards as one single unit and not to consider your own hand separately. In this hand West's jump to 4 ♠ promised four cards in that suit, including at least one high honor. His response to the Blackwood 4 NT bid proved he had the ace of spades. Even if West held four spades to the ace-nothing, there would be a fair play for the slam. It would make if the defenders' four spades split 2-2, and it would also make if the defender on East's left held a singleton king or queen of spades.

For example:

WEST	EAST
♠ A 8 7 6	♠ J 5 4 3 2

East leads the deuce of spades and his left-hand opponent plays the queen (or king). The ace wins and a spade is led back through the other defender, who can take this second round of the suit. But East will win the third round with the jack to clear the suit.

12

Grand Slams

♠ ♡ ◇ ♣

It has already been recommended that you bid a small slam when your chances of making it are about 50 percent or better. However, when you are considering a grand slam your chances should be much better than that. The reason is that the rewards for the small slam are so substantial that they should not be risked unless the grand slam is almost a sure thing.

If someone unexpectedly gave you a million dollars, would you promptly risk it all for the chance of making it two million? Perhaps you would. But if you would go for that kind of a risk I would certainly like to play against you at the bridge table for high stakes. You would be the loser in the long run.

Sometimes, by the use of the Blackwood Convention or the Gerber 4 ♣ bid or cue-bids, you can actually count thirteen sure tricks. I hardly need to point out that this is the ideal situation for getting into a grand slam!

It is not suggested, however, that you wait for this 100 percent certainty. Some modest risk is justified in view of the bonus for the grand slam. But your chances should be considerably more than 50-50. A grand slam that depends on a successful finesse against a king is a bad risk, for example. Or a grand slam that depends for success on six outstanding cards of a certain suit breaking 3-3 (this latter case is less than a 50-50 shot).

Here is a hand where the East player was justified in bidding a grand slam even though he was not absolutely sure he could make it.

WEST (dealer)   EAST
♠ A 4   ♠ K 5 2
♡ K 7 6   ♡ A Q J 10 3
♢ K J 6 5 4   ♢ A 2
♣ K 3 2   ♣ A Q 5

The bidding:

WEST	EAST
1 ♢	2 ♡
3 ♡	4 NT
5 ♢	5 NT
6 ♠	7 ♡
Pass	

East could almost count this hand to thirteen tricks. Using the Blackwood 4 NT and 5 NT bids he found out that his partner had the ace of spades, the king of hearts, the king of diamonds and the king of clubs. Therefore he could count five heart winners, two spade winners, two diamond winners and three winners in clubs. The only flaw was a possible third-round spade loser. But against that possibility East had the following things going for him. West might have only one other spade with his known ace, in which case the third spade from the East hand could be ruffed in dummy. West might have the queen of diamonds along with his known king, and that would furnish a discard for East's third spade. West might have at least three other clubs with his known king, and the fourth club could furnish a spade discard from the East hand. Finally, West could have a five-card diamond suit including only the king, but the fourth or possibly the fifth card in that suit could be established by ruffing in the East hand.

The sum of all these chances made the grand slam an odds-on choice, and East was justified in bidding it. Also, when twelve certain, identifiable tricks are available, it is often true that a squeeze play can be developed. This point adds to our approval of East's decision to go all the way.

Aces and kings are beautiful cards but they are not always the keys to a grand slam—or to any contract, for that matter. Other important factors are suit solidity, honor cards in suits bid by partner and an adequate trump suit.

GRAND-SLAM FORCE

You will occasionally encounter a hand where you are considering putting your partner in a grand slam in his suit. The only suit in which you fear a possible loser is the trump suit itself. Consider the following example:

WEST (dealer)   EAST
♠ A K 2   ♠ J 7 6
♡ ——   ♡ K Q 3
♦ A K Q 10 6 5   ♦ J 2
♣ K 10 5 2   ♣ A 9 8 4 3

West is fairly close to an opening two bid. But he submerges that thought, possibly with some reluctance, and makes the correct opening of 1 ♦. When I have a hand like this it seems that my partner always responds with 1 ♡, but in this case East bid 2 ♣. This call has a musical sound and, justifiably, West immediately starts thinking about a club grand slam. What trick can he lose? His diamonds should take care of East's heart and spade losers, so there is the only remaining question: Is there a loser in the trump suit, clubs? If East has four or five clubs to the ace-nothing, the grand slam will be a bad gamble. But what if he has both ace and queen? Then the grand slam should be practically a laydown, assuming any kind of reasonable distribution of the opposing cards.

West can find out if East has both the ace and the queen of clubs by the use of an artificial bidding gadget known as the *grand slam force*. The Blackwood 4 NT bid is by-passed, and West jumps directly to 5 NT. This bid commands partner to bid seven in his suit *if he has any two of the top three honors in the trump suit* (in this case, clubs). If he has only one of the top three honors, he should bid 6 ♣. If he has no honors at all, West should get a new partner.

Applying the grand slam force to the above example, West bids 5 NT over East's 2 ♣ call. Holding only one of the top club honors, East bids 6 ♣ and the hand is played there. That contract should be made with the expected 3-2 break of the opposing clubs, which will occur about 68 percent of the time. By careful play plus a little luck you might even make it with a 4-1 break.

Now suppose East's hand is:

♠ J 7   ♡ K J 4 3   ◊ 3 2   ♣ A Q 6 4 3

Again West bids 1 ◊, East says 2 ♣ and West bids 5 NT. East's call this time is 7 ♣—because he does have two of the top three honors in the club suit. He may pale a little as he has just barely enough for his first bid of 2 ♣, but he must trust his partner. He is consoled by one thought: If the grand slam is defeated, it is your fault, not his.

In the preceding example the "agreed trump suit" was clubs by inference. However, the situation should be entirely clear to East. The only other suit bid by his side was diamonds. But his partner bid that suit. East did not bid it, he did not raise it and he showed absolutely no interest in it whatsoever. It would be absurd for West to think that East could possibly have two of the three top honors in diamonds, and East knows that. However, when he bid clubs West promptly came to life and jumped all the way to 5 NT. How could West know that the hand would be safe at that high level? Diamonds had not been raised. Obviously, then, West must have a strong holding in clubs. And clubs is a suit in which West *could* reasonably think that his partner might have two high honors. Why? Because he bid the suit. Yes, there should be no misunderstanding about the agreed trump suit in this sequence of bidding.

In many cases where the grand slam force is used, the trump suit is set by direct rather than inferential methods. For example, you bid 1 ♠, partner raises you to 3 ♠ and you then bid 5 NT. This last bid orders partner to bid 7 ♠ if he has ace-king or ace-queen or king-queen in his spade holding. Failing to have one of those holdings, he is expected to bid 6 ♠.

The key that alerts partner to the fact that you are using the grand slam force is the fact that you did *not* bid 4 NT first (Blackwood) or 4 ♣ (Gerber) after a notrump bid.

The grand slam force is a handy gadget, although it must be admitted that it does not come up often. You should use it only when you feel that you *must* find two of the top three trump honors in partner's hand to have a good play for seven. Sometimes, because of the length of your trump suit, you should be in a grand slam even if partner does not have two of the top three honors in the trump suit.

To take an extreme example, suppose your hand contained a spade suit like A 10 9 7 4 3 2. You open the bidding with 1 ♠ and partner raises to 3 ♠. Let's say that by the use of the Blackwood 4 NT and 5 NT bids you find that your partner has the king of spades. Obviously you do not care whether partner has the queen or not. His jump raise has promised four cards in the spade suit, and since the opponents can then have only two they must fall under the ace and king.

To take a somewhat more moderate example, suppose you open the bidding with 1 ♠ and your spade suit is A J 10 6 4 3. Again partner raises to 3 ♠, and the rest of your hand is such that you are considering the possibility of a grand slam. You should not use the grand slam force in a case like this because you should be in a grand slam even if your partner does *not* have both the king and the queen of spades. All you need to find in his hand is the king. His jump raise has promised four spades, giving you a total of ten in the two hands. That leaves only three spades in the hands of the enemy. The ace and king will drop those three cards well over 50 percent of the time.

In addition, you will make 7 ♠ even if all three outstanding cards are in one opponent's hand *if* you make your first spade lead from the "right" side of the table. For example, if you lead the ace first and the three outstanding spades are on your left, you will be home free. Your right-hand opponent will show out and your following lead of the jack will trap the queen. Of course, if your right-hand opponent has three spades, your first lead of the suit would have to be the king from dummy. Left-hand opponent would show out and you could take the proven finesse against the queen on the next round. Which way should you go? I cannot tell you that, but even if you did not think at all you would have a 50 percent chance of playing it right (there are only two opponents who could have three spades). This fact, plus the fact that the ace and king will usually drop three outstanding cards of a suit, puts the odds for the grand slam strongly in your favor.

There is frequently some clue in the bidding or in the choice of the enemy's opening lead or in the fall of the cards that will indicate which opponent is *more likely* to hold all three of the outstanding trumps. There is also the human element to consider. You may observe that one opponent is holding his cards much closer to his chest than usual. He is probably the villain with three of your trumps to the queen.

So do not use the grand slam force just because it is a fancy bid and you want to show that you know about it. Use it only when you think a grand slam will be a bad gamble unless partner has two high trump honors.

VARIATIONS OF THE GRAND-SLAM FORCE

The above description of the bid is what you might call the basic or original meaning. When something like this is devised, variations are promptly conceived in the fertile minds of the "scientists" of the game. Some of these variations are outlined below.

Let's assume that the bidding goes

WEST	EAST
1 ♠	3 ♠
5 NT	?

As mentioned, the 5 NT bid (after skipping 4 NT) is the grand slam force. In this variation, responder (East) acts as follows. With *none* of the three top honors in the agreed trump suit he bids 6 ♣. With one such honor he bids 6 ◇. With two he bids 6 ♡. And with the information thus gained, West can decide

whether or not to bid the grand slam. You will see that this can
be used effectively only when the agreed suit is a major. If the
agreed suit is clubs, for example, your response to the 5 NT bid
might get you beyond the only contract you could make—
namely six clubs.

In another variation the usage depends on the bidding style
of the partnership. If, as many players do, they open only five-
card or longer major suits, then responder needs only three cards
in the bid suit to raise. Suppose the bidding went like this:

WEST	EAST
1 ♠	2 ♠
3 ◇	4 ♣
5 NT	?

Over the 5 NT bid East is required to show the quality of
his holding in the agreed trump suit. With the worst holding he
could possibly have he bids 6 ♣. (The "worst" holding if you are
playing five-card majors would be 4 3 2.) If East has something
better than an absolute minimum trump holding he bids 6 ◇,
and this call also indicates possession of one of the three top
honors. The trump holding here could be K 9 6 or Q 5 4 2.

With a still better trump holding East bids 6 ♡. This shows
two high trump honors, and his holding might be A Q 3 or
K Q 3 2.

Occasionally East will have so many trumps that he thinks a
grand slam will be a reasonable contract even if the partnership
does not have the queen of trumps. For example, suppose this
was the spade holding of the partnership:

WEST	EAST
♠ A 10 9 8 7	♠ K 6 5 4

Here East should bid 6 ◇ to show better-than-minimum
trump support and one high honor. With four spades outstanding, including the queen and jack, the grand slam would be a bad
gamble.

But if the spade holding was like this:

WEST   EAST
♠ A 10 9 8 7   ♠ K 6 5 4 3

East could respond 6 ♠ to the 5 NT bid. The 6 ♠ response says
that East thinks the grand slam can probably be made if West's
trumps are headed by the ace-nothing. He bases this thought on
the idea that with ten trumps in the two hands, the ace and king
will pick up the three trumps held by the enemy. And of course
there is always the possibility that West has opened the bidding
with more than five spades.

If the partnership is bidding four-card majors, the partner
of the 5 NT bidder would have to hold at least six cards in the
agreed trump suit before responding with a 6 ♠ call. Otherwise
he could not be sure the partnership had as many as ten trumps.

Actually, the opportunity for using the grand slam force
appears so rarely that there is not much sense spending a lot of
time on all the variations. If you do choose to do so, however, it
is suggested that you talk it over with your favorite partners and
reach a clear and definite understanding as to what each bid
means. If there is going to be confusion you would be better off if
you had never heard of the bid.

My recommendation is that you use the basic or original
method. This is the simplest way to use it and therefore the least
likely to be forgotten or to cause mix-ups. If there is one place we
do *not* want confusion, it is in the slam zone. There is too much
at stake.

If you think you might forget when partner bids 5 NT, just
try to remember one point, which is the key to the whole thing. If
partner did not *first* bid 4 NT, then his 5 NT call is the grand
slam force.

13

Arithmetic of a Slam

♠   ♡   ◇   ♣

The trick in bridge is to develop a nice sense of balance between risk and reward. Carefully measure your possible gain against your possible loss—particularly when thinking about slam—and you are on your way to being a consistently successful player.

GRAND-SLAM ARITHMETIC

If you do not mind a little arithmetic, look at it this way. If you bid a grand slam in a major suit, vulnerable, that depends on a finesse, you will score 2210 points—500 for the vulnerable game, 210 in trick points and a fat 1500 for the grand slam. This is assuming that your finesse works. If it does not work, however, your loss is *1530 points*—750 for the small slam you could have made, 500 for the vulnerable game, 180 in trick points and the 100-point penalty for going set a trick at the grand slam. To sum up, you have risked losing 1530 points for the chance of gaining 750 points. This is ridiculous.

If you like formulas you should bid a grand slam only when you have twelve sure winners and your final (thirteenth) winner will fail to develop only if you encounter a very bad break—like finding all of the outstanding trumps in one opponent's hand.

We will discuss some further facets of grand-slam bidding later, but for now let us delve into the handling of small slams.

SMALL-SLAM ARITHMETIC

The small slam is a more practical subject than the grand slam for several reasons. First, there is the simple fact that small slams occur much more frequently. Second, with a small slam you are not held to winning all the tricks, so you have time to "move around a little," as the saying goes. And, frequently the winning line of play for twelve tricks involves giving up your one loser at exactly the right time.

This pleasant situation obviously does not exist at a grand slam. And this calls to mind the excited tournament player who berated his partner for going down two at a grand slam. "You could have made it on an endplay!," he shouted.

With these considerations in mind, you should bid a small slam if your chances for making it are only about even. Looking at it mathematically, if you bid a nonvulnerable major-suit slam and go set a trick you have lost a total of 500 points—300 points for the game you could have made, 150 in trick points and a 50-point penalty. If you had made the slam (which, let us say, depended on a successful finesse against one king) you would have gained 500 points, the bonus for the small slam. So that comes out even.

It would be the same if you were vulnerable. If you went set a trick at the slam you would lose a total of 750 points—650 for the game you could have made, plus a 100-point penalty. If you made the slam you would gain 750 points, the bonus for a small slam.

Actually, your chances for gain by risking the small slam are considerably more than cold mathematics would indicate. The very fact that you, as declarer, can see your partner's cards (an advantage denied to your opponents, for they cannot see each other's cards) increases your chances well above 50 percent. Add to this the possibilities of an endplay, a squeeze, a strategic play of some kind, a favorable opening lead or some other defensive error and it becomes evident that you are playing with the odds strongly in your favor if you are depending on only one successful finesse or one favorable suit break.

14

Defending Against Slams

♠　♡　◇　♣

So far we have been discussing *our* slams—how to reach those that will make and how to stay out of those that will not come in. Now, it must be admitted that occasionally our opponents will reach a slam contract. It is then our job to defeat that contract or, at worst, to hold our losses to the minimum.

For this, it pays to get into some arithmetic again. For example, you (or more probably your partner) makes a rather glaring overbid that puts you in a contract of 4 ♡. You are not vulnerable and you go down one. Do you figure your loss is 50 points? Not nearly enough. Your actual loss is 190 points—50 as the penalty for going down one, 90 for the score you could have made by stopping at 3 ♡ and 50 for the theoretical value of a duplicate part score.

Only the 50-point penalty goes on the opponents' score, but the remaining 140 points are there nevertheless and will certainly catch up with you in the long run. For rubber bridge players it should be mentioned, too, that with 90 on a game you enjoy quite a psychological advantage, the extent of which depends on the nature and financial strength of your opponents. Surely you have been in this enviable position and have heard your opponents bid and bid and bid again until you are able to reap a penalty of 300, 500, 700 or more. ("I couldn't let them make a game, partner.") I dearly love stubborn opponents. And rich stubborn opponents are the best.

I am not recommending conservatism—hanging at 3 ♡ when you had a reasonable play for four. (Remember, it was said that going on to four in the above example was a glaring overbid.) Actually you should take some risk in reaching for game contracts, because of the substantial reward involved. But more about that later.

WHEN *NOT* TO DOUBLE

Here is another question to see if you are applying your mathematical skill at the bridge table as well as you do at your office or your bank. Do you double your opponents' small-slam contract when you hold two aces? If you do you had better read on. Let's say that the enemy, not vulnerable, bids to 6 ♡. You have the ace of spades and the ace of clubs. You double, and say you beat them one trick to earn 100 points on your score. But you would have harvested 50 points if you had just passed 6 ♡. Thus your gain is a paltry 50 points. And even if they had been vulnerable your gain would have been only 100 points.

But what if they make it? You will lose a total of 230 points —180 points (doubling the trick score) plus 50 points for making a doubled contract. Thus you are giving odds of more than 4 to 1 that your double will hold up. This is a good way to go broke. And it may be added that unless you are playing against a couple of lunatics, your opponents will *know* that they are off two aces. With Blackwood, Gerber and other ace-asking bids available today, the odds are overwhelming that one of them will be void in a suit where you hold the ace.

It is an old story that has been mentioned previously in this book—with every bid or double that you make you must measure your possible gain against your possible loss, then try to figure what the chances are of your bid being successful.

In the above example you doubled 6♡ holding two aces— eight high-card points. I would much rather double with three high-card points if they consisted of Q J 10 8 in the heart suit. But even then I would pass 6 ♡ because a double might steer the enemy into a contract they can make, such as 6 NT. I would pass the opportunity to double a small slam and take the sure set. After all, when your opponents hold 30 to 35 high-card points and you get a plus score, isn't that victory enough? It should be.

Say your opponent is in a contract of 6 ♡, and with good,

sound, normal play he will go down one. But if you double you warn him of danger and place the outstanding high cards for him. He may resort to good, sound, *abnormal* play—and make the contract. Here you have handed declarer the extra-trick points, the 50-point bonus for making a doubled contract, and the value of the game and the slam as well. Disastrous.

Many players would double a 7 ♠ contract with the following hand, even though spades had been bid strongly by their left-hand opponent:

♠ J 10 9 2   ♡ 5 4 3   ◇ 3 2   ♣ J 10 9 6

The setup in the spade suit could well be:

                    NORTH
                    ♠ 6 5 4
        WEST   EAST
        ♠ ——   ♠ J 10 9 2
                    SOUTH
                    ♠ A K Q 8 7 3

North and South have almost every high card in the deck and no possible loser except in the trump suit. Left to his own devices (not doubled, that is), South will surely lay down the ace of spades at his first opportunity—and he will be down one. He will play the ace of spades because he is a good player and that is the right play. If the four opposing spades are divided 2-2 or 3-1, the grand slam will be a laydown. (And the odds very strongly favor one of those distributions.) Certainly South will not make his first spade lead from dummy and let the four ride if East plays the deuce. If he does, East had better learn to hold up his cards.

But actually East did "show" South his hand. He did it when he said double. Since it was clear that East had no possible winner in hearts, diamonds or clubs, South would know he had J 10 9 2 in spades. What else? It would take nerve for South to lead the four of spades from dummy and let it go if East did

not cover. But he would do it. Actually he would probably not
be faced with that nerve-wracking necessity, because if East was
bad enough to double the grand slam he would probably be bad
enough to play the nine on the first spade lead. South would win
with the queen, West would show out and that would be that.

So do not double a slam because you think you might beat
it one trick. Do not risk a lot to gain a little.

THE LIGHTNER SLAM DOUBLE

Just when you may be beginning to think I recommend
never doubling an opponent's slam bid, I had better get it in the
record that I do recommend your taking that action. But in a
certain specific set of circumstances. And for different reasons
than the ones we have just discussed.

You may know about the *Lightner slam double*—in my
opinion one of the most important and useful contributions ever
made to the game of bridge. This double is an attempt to take
advantage of the unexpected, to cash in on a freak distributional
quirk that the declarer cannot possibly know about. Not until it
is too late, anyway.

It is a command to your partner, the opening leader, to
avoid making his normal opening and to choose an abnormal
lead, usually his longest side suit. In the typical situation you will
hold something like this:

♠ A 2   ♡ 8 7 6 5   ◇ ——   ♣ K J 10 9 4 3 2

The opponents have reached a contract of 6 ♠, with the
declarer sitting on your left. If you pass, your partner is most
likely to lead a club since you have bid that suit somewhere along
the line. Therefore you should *double* 6 ♠. That tells partner not
to lead a club and not to lead a trump but to choose between
hearts and diamonds. Since you have four hearts and no diamonds, chances are very good that partner will have more diamonds than hearts and thus diamonds will stand out as the suit
to lead. Net result: Your ruff and your ace of spades defeats the
contract. Well done!

Remember, when your opponents reach a slam they have been able to exchange a lot of information. In most situations they have established a strong trump suit, have checked on aces and kings, and often have learned about good-fitting cards in each other's side suits. It is seldom that you will beat them with aces and kings because they know you have those cards and they bid the slam anyway. They could well have a void suit where you hold an ace, and the ace opposite a singleton in dummy in the suit where you have a king.

However, in the example shown above there is no way for the declarer to know that the defender on his right was dealt no diamonds at all. The surprise tactic of a Lightner double is a real killer, and there is little that the opponents can do about it. They know what that double means and they might sneak out to 6 NT, which they may or may not make. (It is interesting to note that the opponents will seldom redouble after a Lightner double, for the simple reason that they think they are going down one. Therefore if your partner does get off to the wrong opening lead and the slam is made, your loss is not as great as it might have been.)

If you are thinking hard about this subject you have probably already figured out the monstrous difference between doubling a slam with two aces and doubling a slam with the Lightner double.

In the former case you double because you think your opponents will not make their slam, and you stand to gain 50 or 100 points on your score. In the latter case you double because you think they *will* make it—unless, by some artificial but legal means, *you can get partner off to a certain specific lead*. If you are successful, and you will be most of the time, you will not care much if they forget to put the penalty for the undertrick down on the score. It will be practically nothing compared to your real gain. You have gained the value of the slam, the value of the game plus the trick score, which will average out to well over 1000 points depending on the contract and the vulnerability.

Like everything else in bridge, you cannot expect perfection of the Lightner double. Occasionally you will double your opponents' slam and they will make it. In a rare case declarer may overruff you on the opening trick, being void in the same suit in which you are void. Or your partner may lead a trump or lead your bid suit even though your double has told him that both of those leads are hopeless.

There are times, too, when your partner cannot be sure what lead you want because of the nature and distribution of his hand. In the following situation, for example, he could hardly be criticized if he failed to select the right opening lead:

NORTH (dealer)
♠ K 9 6 5
♡ 9 7 2
◊ A K Q 7 2
♣ Q

WEST
♠ 4 2
♡ 5 4 3
◊ 6 5 4 3
♣ 6 5 4 3

EAST
♠ 8 3
♡ K Q J 10 8 6
◊ ———
♣ A 9 8 7 2

SOUTH
♠ A Q J 10 7
♡ A
◊ J 10 9 8
♣ K J 10

The bidding:

NORTH	EAST	SOUTH	WEST
1 ◊	1 ♡	1 ♠	Pass
2 ♠	Pass	4 NT	Pass
5 ◊	Pass	6 ♠	Pass
Pass	Double	All pass	

East's double says: "Partner, I have bid hearts and that would be your normal lead. But I am telling you not to lead hearts and not to lead trumps but to lead a diamond or a club. I am void in one of those suits and can trump."

West's dilemma is obvious, as he has exactly the same

holdings in diamonds and clubs. If he leads a club, the slam will be made. If he chooses a diamond, it will be down one. The fact that North's first bid was a diamond may make West partial to leading this suit. But it is basically a 50-50 choice. In any case, East's double is sound. If the slam makes, it costs East-West 230 points—180 in trick points and 50 as the bonus for making a doubled contract. However, if West after being clued by the double chooses a diamond, the double would gain 1080 points even if North and South were not vulnerable (500 points for the slam bonus, 300 for the game, 180 in trick points and the 100 point penalty for down one). Remember that without the double North-South would have made the slam, scored all those points, and averted the penalty for going down. If North and South were vulnerable the double would gain 1630 points (saving the 750-point slam bonus, 500 for the game, 180 in trick points plus a 200-point penalty for the undertrick).

Even when the opening leader is in a terrible spot like this, he figures to make the winning choice of leads half the time (because there are only two alternatives to consider). If he merely does that, you can see that the Lightner doubler is well ahead of the game.

Offsetting to some extent the awful situation faced by the West player in the above example, there is also the case where his choice is clear-cut. Suppose, for instance, the bidding went exactly the same and West held:

♠ 4 2   ♡ 5 4 3   ◇ 9 8 6 5 4 3   ♣ 6 5

If East had a void suit, as promised by his double of the slam, surely it would be much more likely to be in diamonds than in clubs.

Although it would be a rare case, it is possible that the opening leader's choice would be 100 percent clear. Suppose that during the auction he had bid hearts and his partner had bid diamonds. The opponents reached a contract of 6 ♠ and his partner doubled. This double of a slam by the partner of the opening leader would be the Lightner double and would say: "Don't lead any suit we have bid and don't lead a trump." The opening leader had better get his hand on a club—or else!

VARIATION OF THE LIGHTNER SLAM DOUBLE

Some players assign a different meaning to the Lightner slam double. They use it to demand the lead of the first side suit bid by the dummy hand. If dummy has bid no side suit but declarer has, then the double demands the lead of declarer's side suit. If declarer has bid two suits other than the eventual trump suit, the double demands the lead of the first side suit bid by declarer. And if neither the dummy nor the declarer has bid any side suit but the defending side has, the double demands the lead of one of the suits that nobody has bid.

Frankly, I abhor that word "demand." It connotes absolute elimination of judgment on the part of the opening leader. Even if it is right I do not like it. As you probably know by now, I am a stubborn and zealous defender of the concept that hard logical thinking and good judgment are more conducive to winning play than the use of a lot of artificial and complicated gadgets that do not work half the time anyway or are forgotten because they come up so seldom.

If you use the double of a slam to demand the lead of the first suit bid by dummy, you are usually depending on high cards to accomplish the set. And this involves considerable danger, as we have already seen.

For example, the setup might be like this:

NORTH (dummy)
◊ K J 8 7 6

EAST (you)
◊ A Q 9

South is the declarer at a contract of 6 ♠, and during the auction North has bid diamonds. You double 6 ♠ demanding the opening lead of a diamond—because that is the first suit bid by dummy. You hope dummy has the king of diamonds and you have ace-queen right over him. However, is there any reason that declarer cannot have a singleton diamond? Or even a void? Or North could have bid diamonds on five to the jack-ten, with declarer holding a guarded king behind you. You have to admit it is no sure thing.

To sum up, it is recommended that you use the Lightner slam double in the manner first outlined—to indicate that you are void in one of the side suits and can win a trick with a lowly card like the deuce of trumps, not with a stray ace or king that declarer probably knows that you have anyway.

On the admirable theory that you will never go broke taking a profit, you must be careful not to use a double when you do *not* want an unusual lead from your partner. Your partner cannot tell that it is *not* a Lightner double.

Suppose your opponents reach 6 ♡ and your hand is:

♠ 5 2   ♡ Q J 10   ◇ A J 10 9 8 5   ♣ 6 5

Early in the auction you had bid diamonds. Here you want partner to make his normal lead which, of course, is a diamond. You hope to win the ace of diamonds and you have a sure trump trick. If you double, hoping to win those two tricks, your partner will (or should) lead a spade or a club, because that is what your double has asked him to do. Declarer may be able to discard his diamond loser on good clubs or spades in the dummy. You cannot have it both ways.

But if your hand was:

♠ 5 4 3 2   ♡ A 3 2   ◇ K Q 10 9 7 3   ♣ ——

you definitely should double as you desperately do *not* want partner to make his normal lead of a diamond. You want him to make the abnormal lead of a club so that you can ruff and get two trump tricks to beat the slam.

DOUBLING A BLACKWOOD RESPONSE

Another bid giving "free" information to partner concerning his choice of opening leads is the double of the response to an opponent's Blackwood 4 NT bid. For example, your opponents are bidding strongly and at one stage your left-hand opponent says 4 NT. His partner responds with 5 ◇, showing one ace. You have a good high-card holding in diamonds and therefore double. This is supposed to represent a weakness of the Blackwood Convention, but the situation comes up so seldom and the rewards of Blackwood are so great and so frequent that this is a "weakness" we can readily endure. And of course the double of a response to an artificial ace-asking bid applies to any slam convention, not just to Blackwood.

A corollary to this double of an opponent's response to 4 NT is that when you do *not* double you say you are not interested in the lead of the suit bid by the responder. This narrows partner's choice of an opening lead to the two other unbid suits.

Admittedly this is getting into pretty deep waters, and you often find that with all of your heavy thinking and delicate inferences the slam turns out to be a laydown and you could have led your hat and not beat it. However, there is no reason why a partnership with the difficult job of defending against a slam should not give each other every possible bit of information, however slight, that might result in a set.

Of course the Lightner slam double cannot be made by the opening leader himself. His doubles of opposing slam bids, if any, have to be made on high cards and trumps. Even when you have what you think is an unpleasant surprise for declarer, it had better be a surprise of the sure-thing variety. As an example of what can happen to you, here is a hand I saw played recently. The West player had what he thought were two sure trump tricks and there was an outside chance that he might win a trick with the king of clubs. When his opponents reached 6 ♠ he doubled in a firm tone.

Neither side vulnerable:

NORTH
♠ K 9 3
♡ K 7 6
◇ 10 5 2
♣ A Q 9 8

WEST   EAST
♠ Q J 10 8   ♠ ———
♡ 10 9 8   ♡ Q J 5 4 3 2
◇ 8 6 3   ◇ 9 7 4
♣ K 10 5   ♣ J 7 6 3

SOUTH (dealer)
♠ A 7 6 5 4 2
♡ A
◇ A K Q J
♣ 4 2

The bidding:

SOUTH	WEST	NORTH	EAST
1 ♠	Pass	2 ♣	Pass
3 ◇	Pass	4 ♠	Pass
4 NT	Pass	5 ◇	Pass
5 NT	Pass	6 ♡	Pass
6 ♠	Double	Pass	Pass
Redouble	Pass	Pass	Pass

The response to South's 4 NT bid told him his side had all the aces. He then bid 5 NT and learned that his partner had two kings. He gave some thought to bidding the grand slam but decided against it, realizing that the missing king might be the king of trumps lying behind his ace. However, when West doubled 6 ♠, South promptly redoubled. His thinking was that West was probably counting on the king and queen of hearts for one trick, and with the lone ace of hearts and plenty of trumps in the closed hand, West was going to get a nasty surprise there.

West led the ten of hearts and South won with the ace. As you see, if the opposing trumps had been split 2-2 the grand slam would have been a laydown (one of the clubs in the closed hand going off on dummy's king of hearts). Or, in a pinch, the club finesse could have been tried and that would have worked.

At trick two South led a low spade, intending to put in the nine from dummy if West played low. But West played the ten, dummy's king won and East showed out. South looked a little pale at this point. His estimate that West's double had been predicated, in part, on the king and queen of hearts was all wrong. He cursed himself silently for redoubling.

But he still had a chance. If West had just the right distribution in the side suits, a trump reduction and an eventual trump endplay was possible. So South ruffed a heart, led a club to finesse the queen and trumped dummy's king of hearts. He cashed the ace, king and queen of diamonds, led his last club to the ace and ruffed a club. West had to follow suit to all of these tricks and it was his turn to pale a little.

Everybody was now down to three cards and this was the position:

NORTH
♠ 9 2
♡ ——
♢ ——
♣ 9

WEST   EAST
♠ Q J 8   ♠ ——
♡ ——   ♡ Q 4
♢ ——   ♢ ——
♣ ——   ♣ J

SOUTH
♠ A 7
♡ ——
♢ J
♣ ——

When South led the jack of diamonds at the eleventh trick, West was a goner. If he played his eight of trumps, dummy would overruff with the nine and the ace of trumps would take the slam-making trick. Actually, he went up with the jack and South discarded the club from dummy. It was then West's lead from the queen-eight of spades into the ace-seven in the closed hand and the nine-deuce in dummy.

So instead of scoring only 180 in trick points, the double made it 360 and the redouble increased it to 720. South also scored 50 points for making a doubled contract, for a grand total gain of 590 points that was directly attributable to West's double. If West had beat the slam a trick he would have gained a pitiful 50 points. So he was laying odds of almost 12 to 1 that he could do it, although he had not thought of it in that way when he doubled. A player who consistently goes against the odds in this fashion does not need a bridge teacher. He needs a psychiatrist.

DOUBLING "ON GENERAL PRINCIPLES"

If you are just getting started at the game you probably suffer from a common malady—a timidity and nervousness about getting all the way up to a slam. You will bid your head off at the level of two or three or even four, but you back off when the auction moves up to the five or six range. You might call it the fear of high places.

There is really no reason why you should be fearful of getting into a contract that requires you to win twelve or thirteen tricks. All you have to do is have the cards for it, and then it is the same as if you were playing something like two clubs. Of course you have to be able to trust your partner. If you cannot, you are entitled to be nervous. I know I am with such a partner. But this lack of trust does not apply to slams alone. You would be nervous with an untrustworthy partner when bidding at the two or three level.

For our purposes here let us assume that you *can* trust your partner. As a bidder, he is not wild and not over-conservative, but just plain good. Now you have another hurdle to overcome. You must develop the ability to realize how good (or bad) your hand may be in relation to your partner's. You base this estimate on partner's bidding and your own cards. Presently you probably overbid your good hands and underbid your bad ones. You mentally ascribe to partner certain strength that his bidding clearly indicates he does not have. To illustrate, you may recall the first few times you played the game. Your partner was your Aunt Emma ("I still prefer auction to contract. I don't care what you say").

The opponents reached a small slam, your partner doubled and they made it. "I doubled on general principles," your partner explained. "I had an ace and a queen and you had to have *something!*" There is the point. You did *not* have to have something. If you passed throughout the auction you figured to have just what you did have—nothing.

Getting away from slam talk for a moment, the principle we are discussing can be well-illustrated in the field of the takeout double. Suppose your right-hand opponent opens the bidding with 1 ◊ and you double, holding:

♠ Q 7 6   ♡ A K 7 5 4   ◊ 6 4   ♣ K J 3

Third hand passes and partner bids 1 ♠. You have a rather nice hand with at least reasonable spade support and a good five-card heart suit. What do you do? You should pass. Keep in mind how weak your partner's hand could be. He has bid because you forced him to do so, and he has not jumped the bidding. He could have four small spades and little in high cards. Spades may not be the best spot and you might be better at hearts, but you cannot afford to find out.

Now suppose you hold this hand:

♠ A 8 5 3   ♡ A J 8 7   ◊ 7 5   ♣ K J 8

Again the opening bid is 1 ◊ on your right and you double. Again partner responds with 1 ♠. This time you have two aces instead of one, and four spades instead of three. What do you do now? Again the answer is pass. You feel a little more comfortable holding four of partner's spades, but you still have only thirteen high-card points. Since partner did not show any

life by jumping the bidding, surely game is out of the question
and you may as well stay as low as possible. If the opponents bid
again you might raise to two spades as a competitive call, but
that would be the limit of your action.

Looking at it the other way around, suppose your left-hand
opponent opens the bidding with 1 ♣, your partner doubles for
takeout and you hold:

♠ A 10 9 7 3 2   ♡ 10 9   ◇ A 10 8 7   ♣ 2

You have only eight high-card points and no kings, queens
or jacks, but I suggest that you bid 4 ♠ without hesitation. This
time you have to figure not how *weak* your partner's hand may
be but how strong it is and how well it figures to fit with yours.
As a matter of fact, partner's hand does not have to be so big in
high cards. His promised strength in spades and hearts (and
probably diamonds, too) will more than make up for any high-
card deficiency. So do not fool around with a bid of two spades,
putting the pressure on partner to land you in the right spot. You
think you can make 4 ♠ opposite a minimum takeout double, so
bid it directly.

Partner's hand could well be:

♠ K Q 5 4   ♡ A 6 4 2   ◇ K 2   ♣ 5 4 3

This is a real minimum, but you will easily make 5 ♠.

Getting back to a slam situation, consider this one. East-
West are vulnerable and the opponents are not. The bidding proceeds as follows:

NORTH (dealer)	EAST	SOUTH	WEST
1 ♣	Pass	1 ♡	2 ♣
2 ♡	Pass	3 ♣	3 ♡
4 ♣	Pass	4 ♡	5 ♣
Pass	?		

East holds:

♠ K 8 6   ♡ 7 4 3 2   ◇ 10 5   ♣ 7 6 5 2

East should bid 6 ♠ without batting an eye. In fact, he probably should have bid 4 ♠ over North's 4 ♣ bid, because by that time East had heard his partner cue-bid both suits bid by the opponents.

This is rather an extreme situation, but the logic of jumping to 6 ♠ stands out a mile. Considering West's bidding, it should be clear that East's king of spades is pure gold—and the ten of diamonds might even be helpful. West has shown a monstrous two-suiter in spades and diamonds. Remember, too, that he might have bid 4 ♠ over South's 4 ♡ bid, if he thought he could make only 4 ♠. He passed up that call and cue-bid again at the five level, vulnerable. Obviously, he is guaranteeing five-odd on the hand—*and he expects to lose to the king of spades!* So East's king of spades figures to be the slam-going trick.

East's hand should be something like:

♠ A Q J 10 7 2   ♡ A   ◇ K Q J 8 6 4   ♣ ——

OPENING LEADS AGAINST SLAMS

It requires courage to delve into a subject like this, for it tends to encourage letters from irate readers . . . "I followed your suggestion and it was the only lead to let declarer make his slam."

With the myriad possible combinations of cards in declarer's hand and the dummy hand, it is obviously impossible to lay down any "rules" for successful leads against slams. In the first place, many slams are ice-cold against *any* lead. So we will toss those out and consider only those cases where the defenders have at least an outside chance to get a plus score—and where that chance will stay alive only if the opening leader makes his best choice.

Although guaranteeing nothing, the fact remains that certain generalities can sensibly be made which will, in the long run, improve your results.

The first suggestion is to keep your spirits up when your opponents bid freely to a small slam. Do not get careless and do not develop that give-up feeling just because you have a very poor hand. Many players get discouraged when the opponents bid a slam and therefore they fail to defend as thoughtfully as they would against a lower contract.

Closely related to the first suggestion is this: Pay close attention to the bidding instead of wallowing in a trough of self-pity. Of course you should always draw inferences from the bidding, but it is especially important when you will be trying to select the killing lead against a slam. If you make a careless or stupid lead, you stand to lose more than if you were defending against something like 2 ◊.

In an effort to lift your morale even further, consider the fact that your opponents are just as apprehensive about the slam as you are. At duplicate bridge they will get a poor score if they make seven (without your help) and also a poor score if they make five. They have to make exactly six—and that is cutting it pretty fine.

Here is an easy example where the right opening lead against a slam stands out clearly—unless you dozed during the bidding. The bidding goes:

SOUTH	NORTH
1 ♠	2 ♡
3 ♡	4 ♠
4 NT	5 ◊
6 ♣	Pass

West probably felt slightly sick when he picked up his hand, which consisted of:

♠ A   ♡ 9 8 6 4   ◊ 8 4 3 2   ♣ 9 8 7 4

However, after hearing the bidding West is almost surely headed for a plus score. He leads a heart against the spade slam. What else? North's 2 ♡ response almost surely promised a five-card suit. South had to have three hearts to raise, and he might have four. Therefore West's partner has either one heart or no hearts at all. Let's assume that East does follow suit to the first heart trick. Declarer wins and leads a trump. West takes the ace and leads another heart, which partner can surely ruff for the setting trick. Isn't it an easy game when you listen to the bidding?

This type of lead against a slam, in which the bidding indicates your partner can ruff, is not such a good prospect when the opening bidder's partner makes his first response in a minor suit. Such a call is often a waiting bid, made with the intension of raising opener's major suit later. It could well be made on a four-card suit or even a three-carder.

For example, if opener bid 1 ♠ and responder held:

♠ K 9 8 2   ♡ 4 3   ◇ 9 8 7 6   ♣ A K J

responder might well say 2 ♣, marking time by telling where his side-suit high-card strength was located and intending to raise spades at his next turn.

However, practically nobody toys with the heart suit in this fashion. If responder bids 2 ♡ over opener's 1 ♠ bid he will almost always have five hearts and possibly more.

The next suggestion on leading against slams is again related to the bidding. Consider what high cards partner is likely to hold. To take an extreme example, suppose you, the opening leader, hold no card higher than an eight spot. Your partner then figures to have several high cards, possibly an ace and a king, or a king and two queens. Looking at it the other way around, suppose you have two kings and a queen. In this case your partner figures to have nothing, unless your opponents are madmen.

There are two general types of leads against a slam—active and passive or, if you prefer, attacking and waiting. Often your choice of an opening lead will depend not only on your own holding but also on what your partner can logically be expected to have. For example, suppose West is on lead against 6 ♠ after the following bidding:

SOUTH	NORTH
1 ♠	3 ♠
4 NT	5 ♡
6 ♠	Pass

West's hand:

♠ 9 8 7   ♡ K 9 2   ◇ K 8 7 3   ♣ Q 9 6

Since West has eight high-card points, it is a reasonable assumption that his partner does not have a face card in his hand. Therefore he could not be expected to hold one of the red queens or the king of clubs, and West's lead away from one of his honor cards could well hand declarer a trick that he could not develop for himself. In a case like this, then, West should not attack as he does not have enough guns. The waiting lead is called for, and the lead of a trump is recommended.

However, suppose West is on opening lead and this was his hand:

♠ J 2   ♡ 9 6 5 4   ◇ 5 4 3   ♣ Q 10 8 3

The bidding:

NORTH (dealer)	EAST	SOUTH	WEST
1 ◇	Pass	1 ♠	Pass
3 ◇	Pass	3 ♠	Pass
4 ♠	Pass	4 NT	Pass
5 ♡	Pass	6 ♠	All pass

This time the recommended lead is a club. West's hand is so weak that his partner figures to have a high card or two. North's strong bidding of diamonds makes it probable that South can get club and heart discards on that suit. West's holding in diamonds indicates that the suit cannot break badly for his opponents. Time is therefore important, and West must take a shot at establishing a club winner before declarer can run away with the hand. West should lead the three of clubs.

Why not a heart lead, thus avoiding leading away from a high honor? Because to be effective that would require East to have two or even three honors in hearts. Why not a spade lead? Because that could be ruinous if East held something like Q 5 4 in spades. The sure trump trick would go up in smoke. While a

club lead could possibly go into declarer's A K J, it is also true
that the lead would probably not lose a trick if East has just *one*
club honor—ace, king or jack.

It bears repeating that choice of an opening lead against a
slam depends to a very considerable extent on the nature of your
opponents' bidding. Occasionally their bidding will clearly ex-
pose their weak spot. Suppose it went like this:

SOUTH	NORTH
1 ♠	3 ♠
4 ♢	4 ♠
5 ♣	5 ♠
6 ♠	Pass

South barreled the bidding and finally reached the slam
practically by himself. North obviously was holding back and
possibly was a little ashamed of his first bid of 3 ♠.

Anyway, it appears that neither of the opponents holds the
ace of hearts. North was given ample opportunity to cue-bid that
card if he had held it. And if South had it, plus the ace of
diamonds and clubs, he probably would have leaped to 6 ♠ over
his partner's 3 ♠ raise, or he would have bid 4 NT instead of
cue-bidding diamonds at his second turn. South could well have
a singleton heart, but a heart would be the best opening lead *no
matter what your holding in the suit*. There should be no hesi-
tancy in leading from a heart holding such as K 4 3 2, a lead
that would be unthinkable if your right-hand opponent had
opened the bidding with 1 ♡.

Unless the bidding indicates a weakness in a certain suit as
just illustrated, it is usually not advisable to lead the top card
from an honor holding that is not solid. For example, the lead of
a queen from Q J 9 or Q J 8 will often find K 10 7 6 in
dummy and a doubleton ace in declarer's hand. Declarer will win
with the ace, finesse dummy's ten on the next lead of the suit and
get a discard on the king. Even worse, dummy may have
K 10 2 and declarer A 4 3. Here declarer may have a sure
third-round loser in the suit, but your lead of the queen hands it
right back to him.

Similarly, the lead of the king from K Q 10 or K Q 9 is dangerous. If your right-hand opponent has bid this suit, your holding figures to be behind his ace (and other cards) and may well win two tricks as long as you do not lead it. If the suit has been bid on your left (the eventual dummy), the lead of the king will help declarer establish the suit for discards. If nobody has bid the suit it is not as dangerous as in the cases just mentioned, but I would still prefer the lead of a queen from Q J 10 in another suit if I had it. With no better lead, the king from K Q 9 would be acceptable, but I would not guarantee that you would not run into J 4 3 in dummy and A 6 5 in declarer's hand.

LEADING AN ACE AGAINST SLAMS

Even among experienced players there is considerable disagreement as to the advisability of leading an ace against a small-slam contract. Of course you have to divide this subject into two sections—making the lead at rubber bridge and making it at duplicate. It is more often right to lead an ace at duplicate because in certain situations your opponents' bidding will make it fairly clear that if you do not cash your ace you will not get it. If you are able to hold your opponents to twelve tricks in their 6 ♠ contract, but let them make a grand slam, you will have earned a nice round zero. You will not get too good a score for holding them to six-odd, as some pairs may not reach the slam, but you will have a lot of company and should get no worse than an average-minus score.

At rubber bridge your main concern is not merely to hold your opponents to their actual contract. It is to defeat the slam. And more often than not, cashing an ace at trick one is not the way to accomplish that. You should be willing to take some risk with your opening lead—and hang the overtrick! The extra trick, if you let them make it, costs only twenty or thirty points. But defeating the slam gains over 1000 points. So the risk is obviously worth it.

I have heard more than one player boast that he *never* leads an ace against a slam. The inference is that it is a cowardly thing to do, a give-up play and certainly a losing play. This is ridiculous. While there are no statistics on the subject, my own observations indicate that the lead of an ace against a slam is a winning lead over half the time *if* you are playing duplicate bridge, *if* your ace is in an unbid suit and *if* your opponents are known to be good, sound bidders.

There are many situations, of course, where the bidding tells you not to lead an ace because that will clearly be the play that declarer hopes you will make. Take this bidding for example:

SOUTH	NORTH
1 ♦	1 ♠
3 ♦	3 ♡
4 ♣	4 NT
5 ♡	6 ♣

East is on lead with the following hand:

♠ 6 5   ♡ 10 9 3 2   ♦ A 3   ♣ Q 6 5 4 3

Leading the ace of diamonds will establish South's (dummy's) long diamond suit. This is exactly what the declarer will try to do as soon as he gets in and clears the trumps. There is no possible chance that your ace of diamonds will go to bed, for North could hardly have a heart (or club) suit on which he could discard five or six diamonds from the board. This bidding sequence screams for a club lead, and if your partner happens to have the king, you have at least a chance to defeat the slam.

In the above example, if you held the ace and a small heart and four small diamonds, again the lead of your ace would be geared to helping declarer. In fact, the ace of hearts might be ruffed in dummy (South), setting up declarer's king or even king, queen, jack.

To sum up, the opening lead of an ace against a slam is likely to be a winning lead only if it is in a suit that your opponents have not bid. Even then, it is likely to gain only if it is quite clear from the bidding that if you do not cash it, declarer's loser or losers in the suit in question can be discarded on a long side suit in dummy. When there is no such evidence, it is usually best not to lead your ace but to fall back on the old axiom that aces are meant to kill opponents' kings.

Occasionally your opponents will reach a small slam without using any conventional ace-asking bids. For example, the bidding might go 1 ♠ on your right, 3 ♠ on your left and 6 ♠ on your right. This is a situation in which it is dangerous to lay down an ace on the opening lead. Again assuming that your opponents are good players and know what they are doing, it is extremely likely that declarer, on your right, has a void in some side suit. Otherwise he would have used the Blackwood 4 NT bid. Your ace might be ruffed by declarer, setting up the king and possibly other high cards in the dummy hand.

LEADING AGAINST A GRAND SLAM

Leading against a grand slam, your best procedure can be summed up in one word: *safety*. If you lead away from a king or queen you will have to look for a new partner for your next game. It is practically impossible for your partner to hold a supporting card. Think back to the bidding and lead the suit in which it appears that your opponents are absolutely solid. This gives them nothing—they have those tricks anyway. Your only hope is that the declarer will err in the play or misguess on a two-way finesse for a queen. There is one other slight hope: your opponents may have grossly overbid and actually have no chance for seven. You may not believe it, but this *has* occurred.

Suppose the opponents' bidding has proceeded like this:

SOUTH (dealer)	NORTH
1 ◊	2 ♠
3 ♠	4 NT
5 ♡	5 NT
6 ♡	7 NT
Pass	

East is on lead against the grand slam, and his hand is:

♠ 876   ♡ J 9 4 3   ♢ 7 6 5   ♣ Q 8 5

This hand is a horror, but we have to make our point. And actually, after the bidding as shown, it is just about all East could expect to hold.

What is the very worst lead East could choose? A club. This is an attacking lead, and attacking leads are not made against grand slams. The queen of clubs is East's only chance to take a trick, and leading a club will probably ruin that chance. A heart is the second worst lead. The holding of four hearts to the jack may be at least a mild irritation to the declarer. But not if a heart is led. As for diamonds, if West has the king of that suit (most unlikely) he does not need a diamond lead to set up the king. If he has the guarded queen, a diamond lead will kill that card. For example, dummy's diamonds might be K J 10 9, with declarer holding A 8 7. If a diamond is led, declarer no longer has to guess about the location of the queen.

So we come down to the only sensible lead against this grand slam—a spade. With North making a jump takeout in that suit and getting an immediate raise from his partner, it is probable that the opponents are solid in spades from the ace to the nine. So East will not gain anything by leading a spade. But, even more important, he will not *lose* anything, either.

When opponents bid a grand slam it may be assumed that they have all the aces—and most of the kings and queens as well. However, they do not necessarily have to hold 37 high-card points between them, as recommended in the textbooks. Occasionally they will reach seven with somewhat less than that, and their bidding could be quite proper. Their distributional advantages could well make up for a modest deficiency in high cards.

In these cases you could hold a king, or even a king and a queen in different suits. Now, at a lower contract, say 3 NT, it might be to your best interests to signal to indicate possession of a high card in a certain suit. The purpose, of course, would be to tell your partner to lead that suit when he got in. I have seen experienced players make such a signal when defending against a grand slam. It is a matter of habit. It is also a very bad habit.

The thing to remember is that your partner *is not going to get the lead!* Or if he does by some fortunate circumstance, the contract is then defeated and you are so happy that you do not care *what* he leads back.

The point is that signaling against a grand slam to indicate possession of a high card cannot help your side. It can only help declarer and tell him how to play the hand. For example, declarer might need one more trick for his contract, depending on his play of a suit in which he has a singleton deuce and dummy has A Q J 3. He can take an immediate finesse against the king or he can lead to the ace and return the queen, hoping to ruff out the king. If you tell him where the king is, his problem is solved.

15

Slam Play

♠ ♡ ◇ ♣

Knowing how and when to bid slams is fine—provided you also know how to take the required number of tricks. Bidding a slam that could make and then failing to make it is a disaster. No book on slams is complete without at least some hints on dummy play. Here are some examples of ways to pick up that extra trick.

LOSING A TRICK TO SET UP A SQUEEZE

In the following hand you will see that South, the declarer at a contract of 6 ♠, has eleven sure winners—seven spade tricks in his own hand, two top diamonds, the ace of clubs and a diamond ruff in the dummy. We do not need to go into the bidding except to say that West was the dealer and opened with 1 ♡.

Let us say that West's opening lead is the king of hearts and that South, an impatient sort, trumps. South can see that his only hope for his twelfth trick is to squeeze West in hearts and clubs. He starts off by picking up the opposing trumps in two leads. Next he cashes the king and ace of diamonds and ruffs his last diamond on the board. He returns to his hand by ruffing a low heart and proceeds to play out the rest of his trumps. This is supposed to embarrass West and force him to discard to his disadvantage.

NORTH
♠ 10 8 4
♡ J 9 6 5 2
◊ K 3
♣ A 7 5

WEST   EAST
♠ 5   ♠ 7 3
♡ A K Q 10 4   ♡ 8 7 3
◊ Q 6 5 4   ◊ J 8 7 2
♣ K J 8   ♣ 10 9 3 2

SOUTH
♠ A K Q J 9 6 2
♡ ——
◊ A 10 9
♣ Q 6 4

However, when South has one trump left, the situation will be:

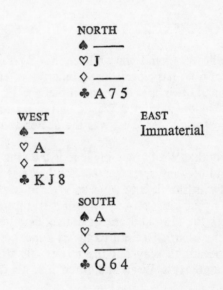

NORTH
♠ ——
♡ J
◊ ——
♣ A 7 5

WEST   EAST
♠ ——   Immaterial
♡ A
◊ ——
♣ K J 8

SOUTH
♠ A
♡ ——
◊ ——
♣ Q 6 4

South leads the ace of trumps, but West is not embarrassed in the least. He simply discards the eight of clubs—he needs only one guard for his king. South now has no play for his contract and loses a club and a heart at the end.

South should have exerted more patience, a wonderful and winning virtue at the bridge table and one, incidentally, that is not practiced enough even by some of our better players.

Specifically, South should have been patient at the very first trick. He should have felt no compulsion to win the *first* twelve tricks. The last twelve, or any twelve, would have enabled him to score the slam. With only eleven tricks in sight and with the advantage of being able to lose one trick, he should have conceded the first one, discarding a low club instead of ruffing and permitting West to win with the king of hearts.

West would have no killing lead to make at trick two, and continuing with the queen of hearts would be as effective as anything else. South would ruff the second heart and then proceed exactly as outlined above. However, when he got down to the point where he had one trump left, the setup would be as follows:

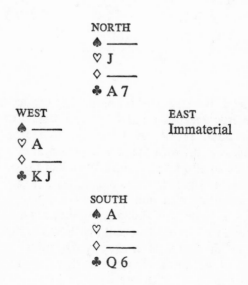

```
                        NORTH
                        ♠ ——
                        ♡ J
                        ♢ ——
                        ♣ A 7

         WEST                              EAST
         ♠ ——                              Immaterial
         ♡ A
         ♢ ——
         ♣ K J

                        SOUTH
                        ♠ A
                        ♡ ——
                        ♢ ——
                        ♣ Q 6
```

This time, when South leads the ace of trumps West's position is hopeless. West could not part with the ace of hearts since dummy's jack is in plain sight. His best shot would be to discard the jack of clubs, as there is at least a possibility that his partner held the queen of that suit. South would then lead the six of clubs to dummy's ace, felling the king and making the queen good for the slam-going trick.

Thus you see what a little patience can do for you. This stratagem of giving up a necessary loser early in the play of a hand is dignified by the somewhat cryptic designation of *rectifying the count.*

LOSING A TRICK TO ENTICE A FAVORABLE LEAD

Occasionally you run into a setup like this:

NORTH
◇ 5 4 3

WEST
◇ K Q 10 6

EAST
◇ 9 8

SOUTH
◇ A J 7 2

West leads the king, and if South takes the ace his jack will be under West's queen-ten and subject to certain death later in the play. So South refuses the trick, but instead of playing the deuce he follows suit with the seven. (Concealing the deuce in this fashion is an effort to convince West that his partner's eight is an encouraging signal from a holding like J 8 2. West is then supposed to lead another diamond right into South's ace-jack.)

When the game was young, say thirty years ago, and defenders tended to be more innocent and trusting, this ruse would work with a fair degree of frequency. In today's sophisticated game it will seldom work. However, even now it is worth trying as there is usually nothing to lose.

There is a tale about the exact setup of cards shown above, and although it may not have actually happened, it does show the mental agility with which some players can slither out of a bad situation.

Our hero was the East player, and when his partner led the king of diamonds he cursed his luck for not having been dealt the nine-deuce. He desperately did not want another diamond lead from his partner, which would probably go into declarer's ace-jack. The deuce (if he had held it) would have encouraged West to shift to some other suit. East's lowest card was the eight, and that would look like an encouraging card, asking for continuation of the diamonds.

East solved his problem neatly, if not with the highest degree of ethics. He dropped the eight of diamonds on the floor and seemed to have some difficulty picking it up. "What is it?" asked West impatiently. "Just a *low* diamond," East replied quietly. . . .

Now, to see if you have been paying attention, consider the following deal in which South is playing a contract of 6 ♠. Just one hint: Do not forget to rectify the count.

NORTH
♠ K J 5
♡ K 5
◇ Q 9 6 5
♣ A 9 5 4

WEST
♠ 4 3 2
♡ J 10 9 7 2
◇ 2
♣ K J 10 8

EAST
♠ 9
♡ 8 6
◇ A K J 10 8 7 4 3
♣ Q 3

SOUTH
♠ A Q 10 8 7 6
♡ A Q 4 3
◇ ——
♣ 7 6 2

The bidding:

EAST (dealer)	SOUTH	WEST	NORTH
4 ◇	4 ♠	Pass	6 ♠
Pass	Pass	Pass	

(If you like double-dummy problems, try to work this out before reading on.)

West led the deuce of diamonds, which appeared to be (and was) a singleton. Dummy played low, East played the ten and South ruffed. South could see six spade winners, three tricks in hearts and the ace of clubs. If he could ruff a heart in dummy that would still be only eleven tricks, one short of the slam. There appeared to be no way to avoid losing two tricks in clubs.

Undaunted, South proceeded as follows. He led a low spade to dummy's jack and noted East's play of the nine. He returned a diamond and ruffed it. Now he led a club and played low from dummy. East won with the queen and his return at this point was immaterial. Actually, he led back his last club, probably hoping to break up a squeeze that South might be planning.

South won the club in dummy, led another diamond and ruffed it. Next he led the queen of spades to dummy's king, returned the last diamond and ruffed it with his last trump, the ace. West's only safe discard on this trick was his last trump.

The situation at this point was:

```
                    NORTH
                    ♠ 5
                    ♡ K 5
                    ◇ ——
                    ♣ 9 5

    WEST                          EAST
    ♠ ——                          ♠ ——
    ♡ J 10 9 7                    ♡ 8 6
    ◇ ——                          ◇ A 8 7
    ♣ K                           ♣ ——

                    SOUTH
                    ♠ ——
                    ♡ A Q 4 3
                    ◇ ——
                    ♣ 7
```

South now led a low heart to dummy's king, played the good five of spades and discarded the seven of clubs from his hand. West's position was then completely hopeless. If he discarded the king of clubs, dummy's nine would be a winner. So he played a heart, reducing his holding in that suit to J 10. South then proceeded to win the last three tricks in the heart suit.

Again patience was rewarded. You do not have to win the *first* twelve tricks at a small slam. Losing a club early in the play was the key to this contract. You can try to make it without losing a club early, but you will be wasting your time.

LOSING A TRICK TO ENSURE THE CONTRACT

Here is another hand to illustrate the eminently comfortable feeling you can enjoy with the knowledge that you can lose one trick and still make a big score.

NORTH
♠ K 10 9
♡ 4 3 2
♢ A K 4 3 2
♣ 5 2

WEST
♠ 7 4
♡ Q J 10 9 8
♢ 6
♣ K 10 8 7 6

EAST
♠ 3 2
♡ 7 5
♢ Q 9 8 7 5
♣ Q J 9 3

SOUTH
♠ A Q J 8 6 5
♡ A K 6
♢ J 10
♣ A 4

South is the declarer at a contract of 6 ♠, and West makes the stand-out safe opening lead of the queen of hearts. South wins with the king and picks up the opposing spades with his ace and queen. Pausing to take stock, he sees that he has a heart loser and a club loser. He has no losers in diamonds, with the ace and king on the board and only two in his hand.

If the opposing diamonds are divided 3-3, South can cash the ace and king, ruff a third round in his hand and thus establish two good diamonds on which to pitch the losing heart and losing club. Strangely, his partner would not praise him for making all thirteen tricks—and his partner would be right. It makes no sense to go against the odds and risk the small slam for an overtrick worth a paltry thirty points, while the play for twelve tricks is a lead-pipe cinch (unless, of course you are playing duplicate and desperately need a top).

After clearing the trumps the play would be to lead the jack of diamonds and let it go if it is not covered by West. This is one of those happy situations where South does not care whether the finesse wins or loses. If it wins, he can park his club or heart loser on dummy's second high diamond. If it loses, he can win any return, cash the ten of diamonds, go to dummy with the king of trumps and discard his heart and club losers on the ace and king of diamonds.

LOSING A TRICK AS A SAFETY MEASURE

Consider that a contract of 6 NT has been reached. In one suit the arrangement is like this:

DECLARER   DUMMY
6 5   A K Q 4 3 2

Declarer has all of the other three suits doubly stopped, for a total of eight tricks and no more. Therefore he must win four tricks in the suit shown above in order to score the slam. The opponents have five cards in that suit, and if these five cards are divided 3-2 he can run the entire suit and make a grand slam with tricks to spare. On the first lead of the suit, however, his right play is the five from his hand and the *deuce* from dummy. This will give up a trick he could have won, but it will ensure the slam in case the defenders' cards in the suit are split 4-1.

If they are divided that way (and assuming there are no entries to dummy in any other suit) declarer will blow the slam by playing dummy's high cards first, hoping for a 3-2 split. Again it is a matter of weighing possible gain against possible losses. The gain would be an extra trick worth thirty points. The loss would be the slam bonus, the game bonus and 190 in trick points.

In taking advantage of the happy fact that you can lose one trick at a small-slam contract and still rack up a big score, you will occasionally encounter a situation where your best shot is to play a certain suit "unnaturally." Suppose this is the trump suit when playing a small slam in hearts:

NORTH
♡ A 8 4

WEST   EAST
♡ Q 10 7 6   ♡ 5

SOUTH (declarer)
♡ K J 9 3 2

Assume that there are no losers in the side suits. In a grand slam, probably the best play would be to lead a low heart to the ace, return a heart and finesse the jack, hoping East had started with three hearts to the queen. In a small slam, however, declarer is (or should be) willing to give up this chance of picking up the queen in the interests of winning twelve tricks.

Declarer can survive the unlucky trump break shown above by playing trumps in a somewhat abnormal manner. The right play is the king of trumps first. When both opponents follow suit with small cards, declarer leads a low heart and plays the eight from the board. If the eight loses to East's ten or queen, declarer is home free. There will be only one trump outstanding and the ace will pick it up.

If the eight wins, the ace will capture the ten and declarer will lose only to the queen. If, on the second trump lead, West puts up the ten, declarer wins with dummy's ace and leads the eight which will knock out the queen. Later declarer's jack will take the seven and again he will have only one loser. This is "moving around" at its finest.

This same handling will be just as successful if Q 10 7 6 in trumps are held by the player on the right. Declarer's king wins the first trump lead. Now when he leads the deuce, his left-hand opponent will show out. So up with dummy's ace and a trump back toward the jack. East will have only the queen and ten left at this point, and only the queen can be a winner. Playing in the manner suggested declarer probably will not win thirteen tricks even if the adverse trumps are divided favorably. On the other hand, he will not win just eleven either.

Consider the following hand in which the South player, as declarer, purposely gave up all hope of winning thirteen tricks to increase his chances of winning twelve.

NORTH
♠ A 10 7 3 2
♡ 10 2
◊ J 9 3 2
♣ 4 2

WEST
♠ K Q J 9
♡ 8 7 6 5 3
◊ Q 5 4
♣ 10

EAST
♠ 8 6 5
♡ ——
◊ 10 8 7 6
♣ Q J 9 7 6 3

SOUTH
♠ 4
♡ A K Q J 9 4
◊ A K
♣ A K 8 5

The bidding:

SOUTH	WEST	NORTH	EAST
2 ♡	Pass	2 NT	Pass
3 ♡	Pass	3 ♠	Pass
4 ♣	Pass	4 ♡	Pass
4 NT	Pass	5 ◇	Pass
6 ♡	Pass	Pass	Pass

Opening lead: king of spades.

At match point duplicate play it is usually best to try to win every possible trick on a hand, even if that involves a slight risk of going set and even if your actual contract is cold.

But, like everything else in the game, there is an exception. When you believe you are in a superior contract and one that may not be reached by your competition, your best plan is to make that contract and forget about trying for an extra trick.

On seeing the dummy in this deal, South's strong impression was that a goodly portion of the field would be in a contract of 6 NT and that reasonably decent defense would defeat that contract.

At notrump there were only eleven winners, and that is what other South players would end up with unless they were favored with the extremely good luck of dropping a doubleton queen of diamonds.

At 6 ♡, however, there was the added chance of ruffing a low club with one of dummy's trumps. South could win all the tricks if the opposing clubs were split 4-3, ruffing both of his small clubs in dummy.

However, he realized that he did not need to win all the tricks to enjoy a good score on the hand. Therefore he made an unusual play to give himself the best chance to make the actual contract.

He won the opening spade lead with dummy's ace and then led a low club to his king. The "natural" play here would be to cash the ace of clubs. But West would ruff the ace and lead a trump. South would end up with a losing club in his hand, for he would be able to ruff only one in dummy.

His play at the third trick was a low club! East won this with the six as West discarded. East returned a spade and South ruffed, led his last low club and overruffed West with dummy's ten of hearts. He then led a trump, picked up West's remaining hearts and claimed the slam.

16

The Humanics of Slam-Bidding

♠ ♡ ◇ ♣

Bridge players are people, which may not come as a bombshell of information. But it is a cold, hard fact that you will win more often if you consider the people as well as the cards. Always keep in mind the varying skills, abilities, temperaments and superstitions of your partners—and your opponents as well.

For example, you are in a rubber bridge game and your partner is by far the weakest player at the table. In this instance, reaching for a slam—even though you have the cards for it—will cost you in the long run. Your best plan is to get the rubber over and acquire a good partner. *Any* profit should satisfy you, not necessarily the maximum potential profit. If you put such a partner in a slam he may well flub it by inadequate or careless play, and he will still be your partner on the next hand. The fact that your bidding was perfect will be no consolation at all. You cannot put *that* on your score sheet. Here is an example of what could happen:

```
                    NORTH
                    ♠ K Q J 4
                    ♡ 4
                    ◇ A K 4
                    ♣ A J 9 6 2

WEST                                    EAST
♠ 10                                    ♠ 7 5 2
♡ 10 9                                  ♡ K J 8 6 5 2
◇ Q 10 9 8 6                            ◇ 7 5
♣ Q 10 7 5 4                            ♣ K 8

                    SOUTH
                    ♠ A 9 8 6 3
                    ♡ A Q 7 3
                    ◇ J 3 2
                    ♣ 3
```

The bidding:

NORTH	EAST	SOUTH	WEST
1 ♣	Pass	1 ♠	Pass
4 ♠	Pass	5 ♡	Pass
6 ♠ ?	Pass	Pass	Pass

North is a good player, his partner is a poor player and his opponents are in the expert class. The first round of bidding is automatic. With a fine partner North's second bid probably would have been 3 ♢, with the plan of raising spades at his next turn. This bidding of two suits, one of them a jump bid, and raising a third would almost surely indicate that North held a singleton heart, a piece of information that might be of inestimable value to South. But in actuality this might be a little too deep for South and could cause him confusion. North therefore decides to make a plain, straightforward bid that cannot possibly be misunderstood—a jump to 4 ♠. Take a sure profit and get out.

Now, however, South invites a small slam with a bid of 5 ♡. He is bidding surprisingly well, and his slam try is fully justified. It is up to North again, and while he considered the people as well as the cards in his previous bids, he now weakens a little. The thought of that big slam bonus lures him on. He bids the slam—and South is going to play it.

Fearing that a lead away from any of his high cards might give up a trick, West got off to the opening lead of the ten of spades. South won in dummy with the king and thought it out. He could see five spade tricks and four top tricks in the other three suits, a total of nine. However, with a singleton opposite an ace in both hearts and clubs it occurred to him that a cross-ruff was the line of play that would bring in a total of twelve tricks. That would net him a total of eight trump winners—plus the four side-suit winners. (He was not the *worst* player in the world!) He was quite correct—a cross-ruff was the right plan—and he embarked on it in the following manner.

At trick two he led to the ace of hearts and then ruffed a heart in dummy. He cashed the ace of clubs and ruffed a club in his hand. He ruffed another heart in dummy, returned another club and ruffed it. On this last trick East was out of clubs and he discarded the five of diamonds. Now South ruffed his last heart with dummy's last trump, and only now did he realize he was in trouble. If he ruffed another club in his hand he would be down to only one trump and there were still two trumps outstanding. Well, he would be all right if both defenders followed twice to diamond leads. That would give him ten tricks, and his two high trumps would make the slam.

He cashed dummy's ace of diamonds and that went through. But when he played the king, East ruffed and returned a good heart. South ruffed the heart and picked up East's last trump. But he had to surrender a diamond trick to West at the end. Down one.

Right plan; wrong execution. The slam was there all right, and North was justified in going on to six—but not with this partner. It is standard practice with good and experienced players to cash out their side-suit winners before starting on a cross-ruff. If South had just cashed dummy's ace and king of diamonds beginning at trick two and then cross-ruffed hearts and clubs, nothing could have prevented him from winning twelve tricks.

Of course, the humanics angle applies to every bid from 1 ♠ up to 7 NT. But it applies with special emphasis and importance to slam contracts, where every trick is vital to success. For example, you get into a contract of something like 3 ♦ with your partner, a weak player, as declarer. He is ice-cold for four but slops a trick and makes only three. You are hurt hardly at all—a mere twenty points lost. Probably you would not even mention to your partner that he should have made another trick.

However, put that same partner in 6 ♠ and let him make only five. You probably would make some brief and pertinent remark about *that* defection, even though, as in the case of the 3 ♦ contract, only one trick was involved. It should be mentioned, however, that if you risk prolonging a rubber when your partner is the weakest player in the game, some of your criticism should be self-criticism. Maybe all of it.

Here is another illustration, and this time North earns an *A* in the humanics of slam-bidding. Again North is playing with a weak partner against good opponents:

NORTH
♠ K 10 4
♡ A K 7 3 2
◇ A 7 6 5
♣ 8

WEST   EAST
♠ 2   ♠ 7 6 3
♡ Q J 9 4   ♡ 10 8 5
◇ K J 3   ◇ Q 8
♣ J 10 9 4 3   ♣ K Q 7 5 2

SOUTH
♠ A Q J 9 8 5
♡ 6
◇ 10 9 4 2
♣ A 6

The bidding:

SOUTH	WEST	NORTH	EAST
1 ♠	Pass	2 ♡	Pass
3 ♠	Pass	4 ♠	All pass

Usually North would surely make some stronger bid than
4 ♠ over partner's jump rebid of 3 ♠. However, this only points
up another danger. This partner may not only play a hand badly,
he may also bid it badly (as he did in this case). With only
eleven high-card points and a singleton in North's hearts, his
correct rebid was a modest 2 ♠. A good six-card suit seems to go
to the head of an inexperienced player.

Anyway, North takes the cautious, sure-profit course and
bids a cowardly (but profitable) 4 ♠. The play then went as
follows: West led the jack of clubs and South won with the ace.
He ruffed his six of clubs in dummy and picked up the opposing
trump in three leads. Next he cashed the ace and king of hearts
and got rid of one diamond from his hand. Then he cashed the
ace of diamonds and conceded two diamond tricks to the opponents. "With an overtrick, partner," he said proudly.

"Beautiful," North replies, rolling his eyes towards the ceiling. No sense in getting South upset by pointing out that he could have made six. There is another hand coming along.

Actually South did not make any horrible mistakes, but he did overlook a line of play, not too complicated, that would have brought in twelve tricks. And of course he would have overlooked it if you had put him in a slam, too.

The play for twelve tricks would be to win the opening club, lead a heart to the ace and ruff a low heart with the eight of spades. Now ruff the six of clubs with dummy's ten of spades. Lead the king of spades, ruff another low heart, then pick up the defenders' trumps. At this stage the king and seven of hearts are good for *two* diamond discards from the closed hand—and the ace of diamonds is in dummy for an entry.

INDEX

Ace, leading of, against slams, 133-35
Aces, asking for
in Blackwood Convention, 5-6
in Gerber 4 ♣ Convention, 19
Asking bids at five level, 37-38

Bidding to slam, 65-112
direct method of, 65-68
economy in, 68-70
humanics of, 151-55
in-between hands and, 93-95
misfits and, 71-73
notrump slams, 85-92
opening 1 NT and, 79-83
scoring and, 111-12, 113
shutout bids and, 97-101
unscientific, 73-75
unusual tries in, 75-77
See also Grand slam force;
Grand slams
Blackwood Convention, 3-17
asking for aces in, 5-6
asking for kings in, 6-7
changes in original, 41-42
cue-bidding before, 38-40
doubling of, 121-25
Gerber 4 ♣ Convention before,
21, 43, 51
grand slams and, 103-4
opponents' interference with, 14-15
playing at 5 NT after, 9-10
premature bidding of, 8-9

queen of trumps and, 15-17
rule of one and two in, 7-8
showing voids and, 10-14
when not to bid, 3-5, 19
whether 4 NT bid is Blackwood,
41-47, 49-51

Controls
counting of, 61-63
defined, 1, 61
Counting
of controls, 61-63
of points vs. playing tricks, 53-60
Cue-bidding, 27-40
Blackwood after, 38-40
to reach 3 NT, 35-37
sequence of, 28-29
to show second-round controls,
29-34
Culbertson, Ely, 79

Defending against slams, 113-37
discard problems, 63
See also Double; Opening leads
against slams
Discard problem of opponents, 63
Distributional values, defined, 54
Double
of Blackwood response, 121-25
"on general principles," 125-28
Lightner slam, 116-21, 122
when *not* to, 114-16
Dummy play, 139-50

Five-level asking bids, 37-38
Freak hands, 74-77
 Lightner slam double and, 116

Game-level jump responses, action
  after, 97-101
Gerber 4 ♣ Convention, 19-25, 42-
  43
 Blackwood for kings after, 21,
   43, 51
 in unusual situations, 24-25
Grand slam force, 105-10
 variations of, 108-10
Grand slams, 103-10
 arithmetic of, 111
 leading against, 135-37
 risks for, 103

High cards
 counting of, 53-63
 secondary advantages of, 63-64

In-between hands, 93-95

Jump responses, game-level, action
  after, 97-101

Kings, asking for, in Blackwood
  Convention, 6-7

Lead
 losing a trick to entice favorable,
   142-45
 See also Opening leads against
   slams
Lightner slam double, 116-21, 122
Losing a trick
 to ensure contract, 145-46
 to entice favorable lead, 142-45
 as safety measure, 146-50
 to set up squeeze, 139-42

McComas, Stanley, 67

Notrump bids
 5 NT in grand slam force, 105-
   10

opening 1 NT, 79-83
3 NT as shutout, 98-99
whether 4 NT is Blackwood, 41-
  47, 49-51
Notrump convention, see Unusual
  notrump convention
Notrump slams, bidding to, 85-92

Opening leads against slams, 128-
  37
 of ace, 133-35
 grand slams, 135-37
Opening 1 NT bid, 79-83
Opponents
 preempt by, 48-49
 See also Defending against slams

Partnership hands
 fitting together of, 53-60
 as misfits, 71-73
Play of slams, 139-50
Playing tricks vs. point count, 53-
  60
Point count
 notrump slams and, 87-88
 vs. playing tricks, 53-60
Points in scoring, 111-12, 113
Preempt, opponents', 48-49

Queen of trumps, Blackwood
  Convention and, 15-17

Roth, Alvin, 41
Rule of one and two, 7-8

Scoring arithmetic and slams, 111-
  12, 113
Shutout bids, 97-101
Squeeze, setting up of, 139-42
Stayman Convention, 25
Stone, Tobias, 41

Time, importance of, 2

Unusual notrump convention, 43-
  47
 originators of, 41